LOOK FOR THE DRIP

And Expect

the

Outpour!

K. Lee

LOOK FOR THE DRIP

And Expect the Outpour!

Published by Krystal Lee Enterprises (KLE Publishing) Copyright © 2024 by K. Lee. All rights reserved. Please send comments and questions:
Krystal Lee Enterprises
770-240-0089 Ext. 1
sales@KLEPub.com
To Reach the Author:
Email: me@drkrystallee.com me@authorklee.com
Web: AuthorKLee.com
Social Media All Channels: @AuthorKLee

Printed in the United States of America.
All rights reserved. No part of this book may be reproduced or transmitted in any form or by any means, electronic or mechanical, including photocopying, recording, or any information storage and retrieval system without written permission of the publisher except for brief quotations used in reviews, written specifically for inclusion in a newspaper, blog, magazine, or academic paper.

ISBN: 978-1-945066-61-0

For the people who have a Word or feel a calling to start a business, write a book, or do something that maybe no one in their family has done, I want to write this book to encourage you! Some of us are catalysts for our family, Joseph, and it is not easy carrying this gift and responsibility when we feel like we need to step in the shoes. This book shares my journey and process that I believe will encourage and inspire you to obtain your goals and calling for your life to the benefit of all who love you.

To my family, friends, and loved ones, thank you for your support. To my Lord and Savior, thank you for the ability to share my testimony and experiences to help others.

May you, the reader, be blessed by reading this book and hearing the stories shared.

K. Lee

LOOK FOR THE DRIP

And Expect the Outpour!

Table of Contents

Introduction	7
It's Going to Rain	11
In A Drought	21
The Mist	33
From a Drizzle to Light Rain	43
The Gray Cloud Hovers	59
The Father Sends the Rain	71
Work Through the Rain	83
That's Not Rain, but Hail	95
Rain that Waters New Life	105
No Clouds in the Sky	117
The Outpour	129
About the Author	135

Scripture from Jeremiah 1:9

Before you were formed in your mother's belly, you were designed with a purpose. I know when we live in this world, many things can come to make us question our existence. The mistakes you make, the truth you find about your imperfection, can shine doubt on if you should be here at times. I want to assure you that you being here is no mistake. You reading this book is also by God's design and on purpose.

When we go to bed at night, we all pray to have sweet dreams. For some of us, this is the best time of our lives because we can explore the places we hope to be in our reality. But what if our reality can be manifested naturally? Would you long to be awake more than you sleep? Would you dream about what life could be instead of closing your eyes to picture a life you don't live?

For many of us, getting over the hump seems to be the problem. We have thought about starting a business, writing a book, working on our core self, and even contemplating spiritual growth. Yet, we don't see the needle move in a meaningful way in one or all of these subjects. What keeps us frozen in time so we don't accomplish the life we could achieve?

Is it because we don't know the way? Do we doubt we deserve it? Or are we so good at lying to ourselves that we start to believe our lives are "all good" as is? The truth is we all have something, if not many things, that we need to work on. Some are obvious to us, and many are silent because we stopped seeing them years ago. We assume this is the way life is supposed to be, and we accept our current condition.

We believe we are meant to live a life of lack. We are born to suffer and feel less than. We worship a God with no power! That others who are doing evil are better off, so why try? Or that the condition we are in, mentally, physically, financially, or socially, is a punishment that we must endure.

This may be true for many people, but not you! You got this book because you want to change one or more of the following areas of your life:

Introduction

- Your Personal Development
- Spiritual Development
- Financial Development - Business Creation or Career Exploration
- You desire to accomplish a goal or dream

Your dream can be many things, such as losing weight, writing a book, going back to school, getting closer to God, getting your joy back, marriage and relationships, having children, etc. No matter your reason for picking up this book. It is my heart's desire to help you get over the hump with some things I learned on my journey that have helped me that can help you too! Okay, enough of this introduction. Let's get to the meat and potatoes!

It is Going to Rain

Scripture from Genesis 6:12-21 (Noah)

How many of us have a secret buried so deep in us we don't know where to find it? We have gifts, talents, ideas, ambitions, or wants, and desires that we don't share because we don't want people to judge us if we don't achieve them. So we pretend that they don't matter, but they nudge us daily in their own special way.

We can see a billboard, a video, a picture, or a person who has or is doing something we want for ourselves. We can brush it off and give one of our many excuses for why we can't. And most days, that would be enough to settle down the restless bear within us for another few hours or days. But the hunger returns, hibernation season is over, and it is time to poke the bear!

When we are not motivated to start on a journey that is long overdue, we do not take it easy on ourselves. We are not doing ourselves a favor but starving our potential. We could be locking our own children out of their legacy and stopping something the Father wants to enter the earth! We are creating an atmosphere of doubt that will choke out our energy and zap our belief quicker than a naysayer who influences our lives.

Have you ever smelled rain in the air, but the wind didn't show signs? The sun was out, or it was just a weird, overcast day that didn't know what to do with itself. Just like that gray space in the sky, a mix of pale white and gray clouds waiting to get a thunderbolt or for a cloud to become full-body gray to mean business, we can fizzle out like flat soda.

Your business journey won't be a straight line, so bury the thought now and have a funeral for it. The good thing is now that your expectations are adjusted, you can grow through your business cycle and enjoy the ride. Nobody knows the turn around each corner. We cannot predict the future or be certain of our end. We can own our actions and put up our best work, but we don't control how people respond.

However, there is a reason for why you are here on Earth! You were not put here by accident. The plans the Good Lord had for bringing you here in your body, origin, hair type, community, to your parents, including your gender, was not by accident.

I know we all have horror stories of how we were treated. We may feel like an outcast in our families, within our school, and in the atmospheres in which we grew up. However, don't let the enemy deceive you.

I was bullied growing up because I was skinny. People used to tell me I was underweight and doubted if my mother fed me, she did. They sent authorities to be sure, too. I remember when they came and checked our fridge, asked her questions, and we were all seated on the couch and interviewed in pairs. They found no fault in our home, so they never came back.

My upbringing wasn't perfect; I didn't have a perfect home, but I did have a loving mother. She had her own battles to fight, and it is true for all of us. We all are imperfect, and though we can easily demand the perfection of another person, we need to be understanding and empathize with others.

My mother is a lot like Noah. She is a prophet and gifted to see many things before they happen in the spirit. She has warned all of us of things that were to come.

Many times, we would listen but didn't trust it all. She had the same stronghold as Noah; she enjoyed drinking. For many months and years of our lives, we were separated because her pain from her mother created gaping holes in her heart.

The only thing to soothe her pain was drinking. She would tell us things. I am sure it was not easy seeing other people's struggles and telling them out of love what you see, all for them to discredit what you are saying.

To look around and see people choose to live a life of hell when it could have been avoided is not easy. Maybe this is also what caused Noah to drink, you think? It doesn't say clearly in the Bible that he warned people of the flood to come.

What it does say is that though this man was not perfect, he was intentional about doing his best to please Yah (God). His heart was right toward God and others. He had the ability to obey the command of God, and the Father gave him an incredible assignment!

Do you know that before you were put on earth, the Father made a plan for your life and destined you for a purpose (Jeremiah 29:11, Jeremiah 1:5)? Have you taken the time yet to embrace your gifts and talents? Have you considered yet that you were not put here to be a decoration for a country and state?

That you were here because there is something in and about you that the world needs! That your children, spouse, and family needs! You and your life matters.

It is Going to Rain

Noah, imperfect, had an assignment, and you do, too! My mother has an assignment for my life, too. In your life, you have imperfect people who are here to help you through their imperfections. Because the Father was pleased, He told Noah I want to use you. I want you to gather the animals and build an ark to protect you and your family for 40 days and 40 nights (Genesis 6:12-21).

I am sure that when he got this assignment, people thought he was crazy as he started to build. When they saw him building a boat on dry land, they shook their head in amazement. Not for his obedience but for his diligence in obeying God when there was no evidence of what he knew was to come. Can the Father tell you something, and you start working without a clear sign? Can you hear that you are called to be great, and you not look at what surrounds you now and doubt it?

How has heartbreak impacted your life? How have the voices, distasteful looks, and hurtful words others have spoken about you impacted your faith? Are you able to see great things ahead for you?

I love how people I know and have had the privilege to work with tell me their childhood stories. Many of them–all of them have had traumatic experiences. They were called names because of their weight (skinny or big) and were made fun of because they were dark (or too light to be black). For being "pretty" or "ugly." To even speaking quietly or loudly. Do you see a pattern?

People who are bored and not focused on their assignment from the Most High will nick-pick and make fun of those who are doing a good work. They will subconsciously cut down others, thinking they are being funny or helping you by being a pessimist. They don't see the damage they are causing. The enemy knows if he can crush your dreams, confidence, and hope when you are young, you will not build a bridge for your family and future legacy. The buck will stop with you, and you will die short of God's promise.

I want to encourage you if you are in a drought. If you are lost on how to go from where you are or how you feel now, to believe for better, know there is more God has for you. My heart grieved for the stories I heard, and in some of their lives, I can see how deliverance still needs to take place.

They have learned how to survive and are saved, but the residue of their past trauma still impacts their lives. I wrote the book series *Embrace Your Crown* to focus on releasing people from the silent bondage they still struggle with. I want to help people understand why they might be in a drought, although it is raining good things, and that it is because something fundamental is missing.

You have to *Embrace Your Crown*! Your purpose, gifts, talent, and the calling on your life– you must know. The drought is real. Some of us are starved for love, attention, confirmation, loyalty, and goodness.

It is Going to Rain

When you step into your purpose and start moving, the strength you need to keep going will be provided as you take steps forward. You cannot quit and say you failed–before you start and that you tried. You have to be mindful of what you want and speak the life you will have going forward.

We are born with natural gifts and talents. Talents born within us are the same as ones learned; we do need to cultivate them. There are natural abilities we can have to draw, speak, and write, but for most of us we need to study to leverage the gift fully. We also can have a gift that we don't recognize as a talent. In this case, how we see our skill set is very important.

Some of the skills I realized I had I didn't see as impressive until school. I was never scared to talk to people. I loved to sing, dance, and be my happy-go-lucky self.

I didn't feel like an outstanding person because of this; it was even normal to me. I thought everyone learned how to talk, hum a tune, and dance. It was rare to find a "black person" who couldn't dance. Do you think that your gifts are just common occurrences?

Growing up, I enjoyed hanging around older people to be helpful and learn from them. My heart for people and the elderly was created by how I was raised. I believe in learning and growing as much as I can. Both of my childhood grandmothers were teachers, and they stressed the importance of education, proper speech, and being ladylike. We couldn't get away with any of the slang and foolishness as they say that other children got away with. If my grandmothers didn't call us out, my mom was sure to tell us to stay in a child's place.

We knew that spot well and learned not to talk back, how to listen when we didn't agree and hold our peace. We could never talk back, and sometimes, that meant having the answer. I laugh now, but I understand the value of that. I needed to learn how to hold my peace because today, as a chaplain and certified coach, I can hold my thoughts and help people find their own answers.

It was better for me to be pulled from psychology and study coaching because I love to see people's growth journey that is self-propelled. The deepest revelation is one that you see as your epiphany, not someone else's diagnosis. What you believe matters, and ultimately, it shapes your world. I believed I was special, but I struggled in some areas, even when I saw my gifts. I had to learn to embrace who I was, and honestly, that took some time.

That level of patience developed in me young fuels my passion for writing and ministering over the years. I like to express myself and help without feeling overbearing or controlling. I don't want to make people feel that their thoughts don't matter or that their viewpoint is wrong if it is simply different. Reading the Bible as a child helped to develop a love and relationship with God. I remember spinning around in my backyard, looking up at the sky, and asking God questions. I didn't hear an audible voice, but I had peace that came over me, and I took that as my answer.

Getting that *Kiss from God* is the mist our hearts need. The still, quiet voice that tells us we are where we need to be and heading in the right direction. Growing up learning the Bible with different teachers and outside the church, I took my studying time as a personal journey. I wanted to learn without walls and religion that push agendas more than the Word of God. I didn't learn churchdom growing up; we didn't go often.

Billy Hall, a father figure to me who passed from cancer, helped me to study with a zeal to understand and apply what I was learning. He would quiz me and ask me questions after I read chapters, and if I couldn't answer them, he would help me out. I do that now with my children when they read.

I put that tip in my books, too, to help us slow down so we can be sure we understand. I remember reading Isaiah and Jeremiah for the first time. I understood nothing I felt. I was like, Lord, you minus well close the Bible because I don't understand any of this.

It was in perfect English, but the revelation was for another time. Sometimes, we arrive at a destination to see it for what it is at that moment. As we live, it has a different meaning that continues to grow year after year. In all my reading, I still have so much to learn. It is a journey that doesn't get old.

Prayer is the same for me. When I started in prayer, I had the quickest and simplest prayers. I am not saying this is wrong or bad for believers who feel that long prayers are necessary. There is a time for everything, for sure.

But embarrassingly, I would fall asleep if I tried to pray too long–especially if I was sitting down or lying on my bed when I first started. I remembered the passage about the Messiah getting on the disciples for going to sleep when He needed them most. I was so convicted that I started to seek out how I could eliminate the temptation to fall asleep. It took time and more living.

Standing also helped a lot! I walk a lot when I pray. Smile. Let's walk to chapter two!

Scripture from 1 Kings Chapter 17

Today, I love prayer, and I feel like I live my day in prayer–that is, in constant communication with God. I think this is why I jumped at the chance to become a chaplain; I enjoy praying a lot. I am a very outgoing person, but I also like silence, seeing water run, and enjoying peace with no drama.

In this gift, I learned to do a lot of things alone. I like writing, accounting, sewing, and crocheting. Being able to handle the quiet permitted me to pursue a career in writing, small business, and sewing.

Although I like numbers, I couldn't do this all day. I needed human interaction. I enjoy people. I needed to balance my interests, which is how I realized them. Next, how to cultivate them becomes the mission? The sprinkles are the gifts. In high school, I won awards for business and creative work. I enjoyed being part of a sewing club in middle school. I joined production programs while being dual enrolled in college. I realized that, while pursuing my talents, they all could have a space in my life.

Do you know there are people right now doing what you dream of and are successful? Some of us are second-guessing our ability to succeed. We are looking at the giants in front of us, and we are back stepping. We are allowing doubt to challenge us and bark in our faces. We shrink the power of God in our lives to be less than what is in the world.

We are not as bold as a lion, but we are cowering like a scared or damaged animal. We are whimpering as we run away, and we say there is a big bad guy who is stopping me. This can be sickness, disease, weight, gender, finances, power, and influence. But, the stops in your life are not because of money, education, and the things we think–it is the mindset we have on whether we can do it or not.

We all have to start from somewhere. Even the epic prophet of the Bible, Elijah, was in a drought. God told him in 1 Kings Chapter 17 to go and give word to King Ahab that there would be a drought for years. "Elijah [...] said unto Ahab, As the Lord God of Israel liveth, before whom I stand, there shall not be dew nor rain these years, but according to my word (v 1)."

In this situation, Elijah was given word that

In A Drought

there would be no rain for years until he prayed for it to return. You know that verse that says to honor your parents so that your days will be long (Exodus 20:12)? What about, if you have a problem with your brother, go and try to settle it before asking for things in prayer (Matt 5:23-24)? My favorite is don't let the sun go down on your anger (Ephesians 4:6).

For some of us, the drought came to our house because someone had wronged us. People who have been eating off your skill set, talents, and goodness, the Father, can choose to judge because of how they treat you. The way we treat others can cause positive relationships to be cut off if we don't know how to treat people.

If you are in a drought, search yourself to see if you might be the cause of the drought. Are you the reason why there is a separation between you and your spouse, you and your children, you and promotion, or you and weight loss? How about between you and writing your book, or better yet, the reason you have drifted away from a strong relationship with God?

Have you been leaning on your own understanding, and that path has led to drought? If you are obedient and your drought comes, it will be for two reasons. One to bless you, or two, to judge you. If it is to bless you, that could mean shifting your direction.

If the Father wants to move us, He can permit

a drought for us to leave. This could be by laying us off, firing us, or even removing our position. When relationships end, He can permit a person to leave you. What God puts together, let no man put asunder–but what we have put together, or what people choose to do, can change our direction also.

    The good news is that if your drought is to bless you–whether you are right or wrong, the Father will do for you what He did for Elijah. He will provide for you even in a famine! Elijah went to a brook that Yah (God) sent him, and he drank and ate what the Father provided. In our day, we can be brought to a friend's house, a shelter, or a stranger's home like the Good Samaritan; He will still provide.

    This time is not meant to curse you, bring you hell, or punish you. It is the opposite. It is to restore you. Help you focus on personal reflection. Dwindle the cares of this life so that you may spend more time with Him. It helps others create a longing for you and miss you. It helps other people come to the realizations they would not have if you were present.

    The drought was to remove distractions and help you focus on what is important for you at this time. Drought can come before the drip and the downpour. In this state, the next best thing is to get a mist from God!

    Now, I have to paint the picture of what to expect if you are being brought to a low place for judgment and punishment. Suppose this is a judgment against you and if you are going to be left on the other side of Noah's ark. Or you are in the land for which Ahab was king and being judged along with him. It wasn't against the king only that the Father judged, but all his people, too. They all went through the drought together. Everyone who goes through what you go through won't have the same story!

The Father can choose to allow people to get to this space for your attention all the same. It is not the Father's will that anyone should perish before receiving many chances to get right with Him (2 Peter 3:9). He gives chances to all people, witches, thieves, murderers, and those with sexual and moral sins. It is His will that we all can be called to repentance.

When the Father sent the drought to Ahab, it was to give him a chance at repentance. Even if the people did not know why Noah was building the ark, they should have peeped game and asked questions. He would have told them, I am sure, whatever the Father desired.

There were numerous people whom the Father had mercy on, and He didn't let them die when He said they would. Hezekiah was supposed to die because he disobeyed God. He invited people who were his enemies to help him fight another enemy instead of relying on God. He underestimated God.

The Father sent him a prophet to let him know since he leaned on a foreign army, that same army knew what he had and would come back and enslave his people. He also told him for his crime, he deserves to die. He repented immediately, and the Father had mercy on him.

Instead of killing him that day, he gave him fifteen more years to live and get it right. The drought came swiftly. He was told he would die. Ahab was told that famine would come. He could have chosen to die, but instead, he chose to get right with the Father.

The people who could have been on Noah's Ark if only they could find conviction. Although many were getting married and enjoying the things of life, they were not sensitive that the Love of God was missing from their lives. I am sure they were doing everything people do to stay busy: working sun up to sun down, sleeping around, having a murderous heart, back-stabbing, and the list went on.

The Father said the people were evil, and they all thought about violence and death. They were all narcissistic and doing what they wanted to get ahead. They had zero regard for each other and even less for God, the Creator of everything.

If you are headed down a hell path, it is like God to call you back to Him. I remember my drought came a few times in my life. Oftentimes, the drought came because of something I was believing or doing. I just dropped a nugget here: A drought can come many times in your life, and no two droughts have to be alike. They can be for different reasons, so check

In A Drought

your life before you assume what it is for.

I had a drought in my relationships because I wanted things to work out with a man who was not good for me. We had plans to get married, we had a child together, but his lifestyle was atrocious. He was into a lifestyle that was counterproductive to what I should have been doing in life. I want things to work out because of how much I had invested, but no matter how many times we had conversations, they all ended in the same actions over six years.

When I would reconnect with him, my finances would crash. My business would stall. My energy would swing from left to right. I wasn't sure of where the ground was beneath my feet. So it was terrible. Suffering for no reason is just suffering.

How many of you know that if you are unequally yolked, the two of you will not walk together, and you will never work? That relationship will cause more pain and damage. It is essentially a relationship on soul ties and not purpose. It can be hard to look at what you permitted access to your destiny and not have some regrets or strong emotions when it doesn't work out. When we cut toxic things from our lives, when it scatters, we can still feel empty.

When the Father comes in and heals a person, He cleans out evil spirits. But, like how when you clean something out, it won't be vacant for long. Other things will want to use that same space for something else.

Evil spirits want to come back, like how toxic people desire to come back into your life. You can feel lonely to see nothing where there used to be something or someone. Sometimes, in this weak space, we can extend our drought further. If you find yourself in a cyclical situation of sending away pain and bringing it back, the word is being stolen from you.

Have you heard of the parable about the seeds sown? Yashua (Jesus) preached about the seeds that were sowed on different grounds. Some seeds were sown on good ground, fertile, and others on stony, rocky, and on top of the ground! Where the word was on the surface, it was burned up by the sun. Where it fell on rocks and stony ground, it had no roots.

Essentially, the seed is the Word. When we hear a word that can change our lives, when we realize the truth, we must work to keep the word in our memory. We must till the ground, water it become familiar with it, and keep it in an atmosphere for the plant to come forth.

Sometimes, the drought could mean the most important action is happening underground. When we get a confirmation of a word of confidence to improve our lives, don't think that because there is no action on top, we have made a mistake. Don't think that because that person is gone, and now you are alone, you have nothing. The good work is happening within you!

In A Drought

It wasn't until I cut ties that I felt at peace. The drought brings a restless spirit. You might have peace for a night, but you don't see continual peace for where you are.

I knew it wouldn't work, but I still tried to make it work! Have you ever been there? Where the money they had, the provision that should have been there, the car they drove, and the sky-rise they lived in were not the cost of your soul.

My mind, will, and emotions were in hell! I would look at the skyline and pray to Yah many mornings, and I would have peace when I did. When he and I had conversations about ministry, the Bible, and Yah (God), it was great.

I could see his heart wanting to move, but I would see his actions do the opposite. I had to learn to create healthy boundaries with him. I had to learn that not every person who wanted to be with me and could do things that seemed right on the outside had the best intentions for my soul.

I learned he was always supposed to be a ministry connection and not a love connection. If I had treated him as I should have in my life, I would not have gone through several drought periods in this sense. In this case, the drought was a rebuke, a correction by a loving Father–but because I am His child, He had mercy on me and kept me still.

The car that I lost, when I changed my direction, He gave it back and paid it off. When I cut him off and stayed away, my debts were cleared. When I continued to go it alone because he never helped with our daughter, he did not–not even once, make a child support payment, although he makes undisclosed amounts of money and entertains with entertainers and high society. He drives luxury cars and owns hotel buildings and stores, yet he has never looked back to help me with anything.

It has been me and Yah raising Zoe. So, He is still providing for me even during what some may call a drought because of her father's lack of support. But how many of you know? I don't feel the drought because I am at the brook where the Father has fed us, clothed us, and provided transportation and food.

My dreams are within reach and manifesting! I am doing my calling, and I am doing it without the help of my children's father. I don't brag about this, and I don't celebrate their lack of responsibility. I share this to show others (maybe you) that if this, too, is your story, don't think this drought will stop the overflow!

There is still more, and as I have learned to do, we are going to press on. You will get past drought if you accept the Hand of God, which removes bitterness, malice, rage, the spirit of betrayal, and injustice. He allows me to remain free of strongholds that could have easily caused me to learn nothing from my drought.

In A Drought

I thank Yah that I was returned to my right mind, and I pray for my children's fathers who are still lost, bound in a world of hell that I am glad I don't have to take part in. Sometimes, it is in the drought that we are being made free so that we can build on a better foundation that can withstand winds, storms, challenges, heartbreak, good times, and hard times. Let's get past the drought!

The Mist

Chapter 3

Scripture from Isaiah 9:3

What about the mist? Have you ever visited a theme park and stood outside in a hot line? I am talking about 90 degrees in humid weather, that kind of heat! If you have been to these parks, you will find fans of all sizes set to blow wind in the direction of the people standing in line.

This wind is sent to encourage you not to worry so much about how slow or fast the line is moving. The breeze is welcomed because it cools you off when you are hot. During colder months, it might be a heater, depending on where you live, but the effect is the same: you get relief.

When you are in a drought, you pray for a breakthrough. I remember when I was leaving my stepdad's house. It was an awkward time because he was very possessive and wanted things his way. He could not see your pain, frustration, or desperation to be free. He only saw what he wanted, and if that was your mind, your body, your joy, your laughter, your eyes, he didn't care about taking it all.

I prayed many nights to get away from that house, but some of my prayers were dark. I prayed to leave by ending up in a hospital, by death, if that was okay with God. I never thought of suicide; that was a sin, but I did think if this was life, I didn't want it.

I don't want to go through this all my life and be stuck here. I felt stuck when I was living with him. My mom was battling her own demons and couldn't help.

Her stepfather was a pedophile, too, so it put me between a rock and a hard place. I couldn't think of burdening others, and honestly, I was ashamed of the situation. It is strange how the abused can still have a heart and pray for the abuser.

In this situation, I was in a drought. If it were not for the Lord, I honestly wouldn't have made it. I felt low and was fighting the good in me, including anything physical. I was hiding, thinking if I put up good grades, let my hair go, and wore unappealing clothes, I would just blend into the background. I underestimated how much the light of God would shine on a lamp stand, not competing for His glory.

I never wanted to be special, but I needed to

know that I was. I felt ashamed of my progress and what I had to bring to life. I didn't think of getting married because my relationship was polluted. I didn't have a balanced story to write.

I remember being so ashamed of this part of my life that I didn't include it in my first book either. Sometimes, in our drought, we can think of hiding. We can plan to run away, believing that running or getting distracted with work, grades, cars, houses, money, and things will chase away the deep-rooted seed of shame.

I needed a mist or a mighty fan to blow in my direction. That initial mist was me finding my gifts! When you don't get the gentle nudges to remind you that your value is more than your hair, your clothes, your sexual appetite, and the things you can do for somebody, you get a gentle breeze that brings relief.

When you are under incredible amounts of pressure, heat, you can breathe when you have moments to express yourself. There is power in realizing how you feel so that you can have an honest healing process. We all have to get real about what is bothering us at some point, but while we are awaiting deliverance, keeping busy on things that are positive helps!

I started going hard in school. Before this trauma, I was a "C-level student." I was told I would be held back in second grade because they felt the work was too hard for me. I struggled to read growing up.

Funny, now I am a writer for a living! Haha, the gifts of God. I remember when my mom told me, "You ain't stupid. You can read. If you fail that grade, you are getting a whooping."

That was enough for me to get my life together, and I learned to read and passed second grade–but I was no scholar. If I had allowed my low grades or my drought of falling below perfection to damage and derail my vision to succeed somewhere else, I could have never believed Yah (God) to get me here! What are you stuck on that has held you back from *Embracing Your Crown*?

I wrote this series, and the first book is still very close to my heart. It's a favorite because I was the most free when writing this series. I encourage you to read it. Anyhow, I went for pulling out the best in me with academics.

I signed up for anything that could keep me out of the house and make good use of my time. As a teenager, I was building strategies for how I would escape. I knew college was the ticket out. I also knew I had no money, so I needed every scholarship and free money somebody would give me.

I got into honors courses in high school after ninth grade. I heard about attending college while still in high school, and I jumped on it. I was getting good grades, and the mist was great. But I was still in line like everyone else, buying my time in high school.

I took every course I could entering tenth grade on campus. I bought my first car cash from a dealer after working a summer. As soon as I had a license, I had a car, and I paid my phone bill with my own money and car insurance at sixteen. I didn't want to owe anyone anything–especially my stepdad.

I started to feel like life was looking up for me. I earned As in all of my classes–except math ones, haha, in high school and college. I was super proud of myself, and I paid no mind to the judgmental comments my stepfather made. He would say things like, "So, you think you are better than me now?" I would always reply, "No, I just want to be something."

He couldn't argue with me, although he tried his best. I knew how to walk the line and still make life happen. He would spy on me to see if I was really in college, and every time he found me where I said I would be because that is where I was! Sometimes, you just have to make people a believer that what you want, you are not afraid to work for it. You are not afraid to believe for it–even when you are going through hell, you will fight rather than lay passively and die.

It would have been too easy to die, I guess. I wanted to prove I could do this. As I reached my senior year and stood ready to graduate, I wanted to finish college with honors. I could have finished both high school and earned my AA degree at the same time.

But I wanted to be great, so I went to school for one more semester and graduated with honors for my AA degree. The truth, I was glad I got my degree because that meant I could get into any college. I didn't have to worry about SAT scores and ACT because my degree opened the doors of the schools I was thinking about.

I didn't go straight to a four-year college after graduating. I never had the on-campus life because I needed to move! I moved out as soon as I could at 18 and never looked back.

I wanted to help a family member too who had a hard life like I had, and I couldn't leave her and go off to live on a college campus. I wanted to always keep a room and space for her if she ever needed me. I was there for her, and I am so proud of what she has achieved for herself and her children now.

We have to believe we have value even when no one around us confirms it. It took me several weeks to get a job when I had all of the bills I had accumulated living on my own. When I got my new life, I quit my old job and didn't go to any of the places I had been before. I essentially disappeared from the life I knew. I felt free, but I also felt troubled because I was running out of savings.

The Mist

I needed more than a mist. I needed a drizzle, a light rain, or something to help me. I always had a prayer life. I didn't know God in the Bible sense. At this time I knew Him in the sense that He is good, busy, and watching over the earth.

I would ask things in my prayers and always include a way for the Father to get out in case it didn't happen. I couldn't afford not to believe in Him. He was all I had, and ironically, I didn't know Him all that well. But I needed what I knew!

Sometimes, we don't have all the facts and are not completely equipped for our journey, we feel. What I was believing God for, He always answered. I cannot say He didn't make a way of escape for me. I just didn't like the direction or didn't want to leave others behind.

I was ready, but those who I thought needed me did not leave with me. I stayed for them, and in turn, they stayed after I was forced to leave. So, my staying late was a sacrifice I made and not obedience. I suffered because of my own fault and not because I had to. The Bible says He prefers obedience more than sacrifice (1 Samuel 15:22).

It's amazing how we think we need to suffer to help someone else. We think I need to struggle so someone else won't have to. I needed to kick that theology as soon as possible.

When I was eighteen, I learned that. I figured

it out after bumping my head, and I never wanted to repeat it. After my childhood trauma, I have never accepted another abusive relationship in my life since! I know sometimes, when we go through abuse, we may associate abuse with love, care, and a healthy relationship. Nope! I was not going down that road at all.

I wasn't perfect in my pursuit of love, of course, but that was never an issue I had. We can not apologize for letting people go who are a sacrifice to be in alignment with God through obedience. The Father doesn't get glory out of our pain. He gets glory out of our growth. We may go through blunders and hard times, but what we learn and how we commit to His standard for our lives matter.

I got three jobs in about three weeks. I was applying to jobs left and right. At this time, I was not yet in a trade school for production. I was working to pay my bills. I was handling the bills, too, but I felt empty.

The drizzle had come, but it wasn't enough. My life had successful bits in it. I was free, I had money, I had my own place, but I was tired. I worked every hour, it seemed, for ten hours plus each day. I was lucky to have a full day off even though my positions were all part-time.

Leaving one job for the next was getting old, and I wasn't seeing any growth. Sometimes the money can help us to forget about the purpose of our

The Mist

lives. The drizzle can give us enough to feel the rain and see our success, but it robs us of the outpour if we settle.

Don't settle was all I seemed to have heard, so I went to enroll in school. I didn't know what the financial picture was at this time for me to attend. I was keeping up with my bills, but school would have been another bill if I missed out on grants and scholarships.

I broke down in the office when she gave me the bill. She said with my grant money, I was still short of what I needed by a few thousand dollars. I prayed while I heard the news that this would not be the final say. I wasn't sure where this money would come from, but if the Father wanted me to attend, I would make it somehow. I kept on working my jobs and praying as I lay awake in my bed.

I had no one to turn to. I lost connection with my mother, and my siblings and family members, I didn't rely on. I saved them from going through with me. Some lessons I knew I had to learn alone, and I was okay with that.

I didn't hide from family, though. It was a blessing when I got the call about my enrollment. She told me, "I found the money," and I had three sources of funding. She looked out for me so well, that I was getting paid a small fee to attend school!

From a Drizzle to Light Rain

Scripture from 2 Corinthians 9:10

Again, the Father provided and increased me. While attending school, I couldn't keep up with my jobs. One by one, I quit a job to maintain my grades. When I got down to one job, I stayed there until I landed my first major position in life thus far. I was told that a prominent television station was looking for a paid intern or skilled person from the school. There were about twenty of us who applied, and I might have been the youngest.

Sometimes, you have to be like David and stand up to your Goliath, knowing you have power in whatever you have. I didn't have a resume like the others. I didn't have my certificate yet!

I was still in the program and working about six days a week. But I applied and got an interview.

The interview wasn't difficult. Many of the things I knew how to do was because I was playing around with computers on my own time since college after taking production electives for my AA degree.

I have always had a love for production and storytelling. I didn't think I was going to be a writer at all times of my life. In the beginning, I wanted to be the talent, but that transitioned a lot when I reached production school. I wanted to become a producer/director and then a writer.

My interest in being out front shifted to the shadows, and I didn't mind it. I ended up getting that job! There was a shortlist, and they tried out another staff member from the school with me, but he fell off in productivity and stopped showing up weeks into his engagement.

I worked as much as I could to learn and grow. I was making $125 a day for my time, and it was going well. I did this for several months and even was able to work for a non-profit on my lunch breaks. I love art, so I worked for an art program. A drought came, and they cut the program. I loved working with the children, artists, and the public as an art tour guide of folk art.

So, about three months in, I was alerted of a change in policy. I had to incorporate as a business to keep working for them or become an employee. I loved my freedom, so starting my business seemed like the right thing.

From a Drizzle to Light Rain

I incorporated my business by following the prompts online. It was surprisingly easy to do. I got an email and a letter in the mail to confirm my status as a business owner. I was excited to turn my docs in and receive a pay bump for my daily rate.

My days increased soon to working five days a week from three. I was able to quit my last job and work full-time for the station. I graduated with high grades and was the only female left in the program to finish.

We started the class with about twelve students (two women). I finished with about five others. Staying in when others jump ship is critical to reaching the outpour. Many will start the race with you, but not all of them will finish.

Somehow, they got lost and stopped seeing graduation as part of their process–even if it was part of it. What we start out believing is good; that is the mist. What we continue to believe can bring the drizzle. The more you pursue your future and what you hope to accomplish, the more you can believe in the future you want to have.

Have you noticed that if you have a bottle that doesn't have the top on all the way, it will drip around the cap? When we think to bottle our talents, believing we are not enough, we can leak frustration, feelings of inadequacy, and doubt our talents or if we are ready to step out into our vision.

After I started this first business, I began to look for other gigs outside of the station. I thought of filming weddings and birthdays, essentially being an event videographer. I could film, edit, and plan the event.

If I needed to hire someone, I knew how to work around the business implications of that, too. When I started this company, I was charging $250 for a four-hour event. I made a short video, and it didn't matter if it was a birthday or a wedding.

The first job I got was for filming a Jehovah's Witness wedding. After the first one, I knew I would not film another. The sermon was underwhelming and it was different from what I was used to.

So I was confident that I filmed everything well, but the client didn't have the full payment for the job. I felt bad about keeping the footage, so I gave it to them. That is also why I didn't want to deal with any of their referrals.

In business, referrals and working with clients are a two-way street. Not everyone is your ideal client. Some people can be projects you want to do at no cost, and if a client needs that, I think they should be upfront about it so that you both can make a choice about how to work together in good faith.

A few months after this job, I landed a job with a fun and punchy German family. Mr. and Mrs. Adams were so different but so perfect together. Mr.

From a Drizzle to Light Rain

Adams was an engineer who worked for a well-established company. His wife worked as a midwife in Germany, but the US didn't recognize her training.

She didn't practice here professionally. She was just helpful to her children, friends, and family who wanted her help during their pregnancy. I remember meeting Mr. Adams out in public, and he was dancing! I thought it odd to see a fairly tall man dancing, moving his feet, and singing his own song as I walked by.

I said, "Hey, you are a pretty good dancer." He replied, "Thanks. I love to dance. My wife is not much of a dancer, but maybe that will change."

"I am sure you can teach her."

"So, are you a dancer?"

"Yes, I dance to a lot of different music. I love ballroom dancing, so I get it."

"Oh, really!" he says as he steps closer to me. "Do you think my wife and I could come where you go? I've been meaning to get out and dance a bit."

I started going to a social event center with seniors. I enjoyed hanging out with older people all of my life. So, Dancing with the Oldies was one of my favorite things to do. I also thought the title of the event was fitting and clever. So, I met him and his wife when they came to the weekly Wednesday event. They were such a dynamic pair because Mrs. Adams was firm and kind, but you can tell she was no joke.

She seldom laughed. She talked straight, and her jokes were unintentional. I would laugh because her take on life was so blunt and I enjoyed her matter-of-fact opinion. She ended it with a funny statement and would shake her head and wink one eye. We danced a few times, and they invited me to go on a hike with them.

Now, you know, melinated people don't usually go hiking when you look at the bulk of us. So I asked, "Are you joking?"

Mr. Adams smiles and says, "Of course not. It is fun to be out in the sun and catch an early morning hike." He smiles a lot when he talks and has a childlike personality. He is brilliant but so approachable and humbled. I am grateful that they both took a liking to me, and so did their two daughters.

Mrs. Helga says, "No, Jim. She is saying she might not want to go hiking. Not everyone wants to go walking through the woods. There are plenty of ways to get sun than walking around sticks." I laughed because she said perhaps what I was thinking, but again, very blunt. Then I said, "If I don't have to worry about a snake, I'm in."

"Oh great, Krystal. You are just going to love it. You can meet our girls too!" We all went on a hike, and I felt like I was one of the characters in the nursery rhyme "Where Going on A Bear Hunt." It was funny to see them in their hiking gear and walking sticks. He told me the stick was for the snakes. Again, "Are you serious?" He replies, "Oh, yes. This is enough, though."

Nervously, I pressed on, and Mrs. Adams gave me a look of "See, I told you so" without saying a word. Her emotions were always on her face, and I could only respond with a laugh. She started to laugh with me. I'm not sure if she started to believe me when I told her she was unbelievably funny or if she enjoyed my laugh like I loved her sarcasm.

We walked the trail for about two hours, and I had the best time. I wanted to keep hiking after that day, and many times in my life, I have taken walking trails to explore the safe outdoors. On this hike, I also met my second client. One of his daughters were getting married, and he asked me to film it. His daughter was a musician, and so was her husband. They both majored in music in college.

They had the cutest little girl, and he played the tuba! For the wedding, he played a bit as a surprise, and she jumped in also. The wedding was a nice outdoor wedding at a gazebo. I loved the simplicity and the nature. It was so them, and the footage was awesome. I made $800 on this project.

My next project was a wedding for a Nigerian family. It was a two-day affair. They had a traditional wedding and a formal one. The traditional wedding was amazing to witness. She had two dresses, a traditional dress with matching jewelry and a white dress for the church the next day.

The traditional dress had this orange jewelry that was gorgeous and heavy. The head wraps people wore were stunning. I loved hair wraps from that moment, even though I didn't know how to tie them.

I filmed the bride in preparation, and when she was ready, I headed out to the living room to film some of the negotiations. I came out to the living room and witnessed a dowry being paid. In their culture, the man has to pay the father to marry the daughter. I thought that was odd because we were in 2005 or 2006! I had never seen a culture like theirs, but I love their concepts.

The man was putting what looked like walnuts or rocks in a bowl. Each rock in the bowl represented $10k (if I was mistaken). I tried to make sure I heard them right, and they did repeat the same amount. My mouth almost dropped. But I played cool because I had to film it. Even with their accents, their English was clear enough to me.

The father even said, "Let me give you some of these back so you can take care of my daughter." (He initially had eight stones in the bowl!) The father and the uncles, who were also at the table, laughed jokingly but seriously. He shook his head and said to him as he put each rock in, "No, not enough." The

From a Drizzle to Light Rain
man talked with his family and kept adding stones.

He literally had beads of sweat on his forehead. What I liked was what the dad did. He kept saying why what he put in the pot wasn't enough based on how he cared for her. He mentioned her college, her shelter, her car, and how he had to be able to afford her. The crazy part is if he stopped, the wedding would be off! The room felt that man's nerves.

I think it was this occasion that made my $1,300 contract turn into $750. She paid a deposit but never made the second payment. She said they were out of money! I told her it was okay; I really enjoyed the celebration and not to worry about it.

My footage was better than the guy her husband had hired, so she wanted to pay me to finish it. I gave her the footage and told her to have the guys edit mine, and she would be fine. So yeah, he gave her daddy $60k before the traditional wedding could start.

I like Nigerian events, though. I once filmed a birthday party for an only son. They wanted something really simple, and I charged $500 for the event. I was there for only two to three hours.

The wife was a nurse and had a business with other nurses working for her. She drove a Mercedes SUV, her husband had one, and they stayed in a large estate in a very posh area. I hadn't seen anybody of color live like this up until that day.

She was super kind, and she gave me a referral for another film project that I did without hesitation. She was throwing a birthday party for their one-year-old son. She spent $10k on this birthday party. She rented out a huge room that had a stage. She hired a live band (who charged $5k to play), she had two tables of food, and everybody showed up like two and three hours late.

At first, I was about to leave because she had told me to. But I told her, "No, let me stay another hour. I felt bad that I hadn't filmed anything but the food and decorations. And a little of the band." When people started coming, it was about 60 people who came. The band picked up their step, and they stayed until 3am or 4am playing all night.

I couldn't hang with them, but seeing them shower dollars over people's heads as they danced was so cute. The band had money stacked in ten piles that people were dropping on the stage. Although this family spent $10k on the party, they picked up garbage bags full of money. At the end of the party, I left around 10pm; they had $25k cash! If you can party with Nigerians, go for the experience and the fun!

Apparently, many people in the room were multi-millionaires, and they didn't stop giving the whole night. Everybody was getting and giving money. It was one of the funniest times I had. She

From a Drizzle to Light Rain
told me to dance and get some money, but I was professional. I filmed the event, made sure people had a good time, and I left. She gave me a tip of like $500.

Sometimes, the sprinkle of goodness comes when you do things with a pure heart. When you treat people right, your business will grow when you have people who like and trust you. I worked on another wedding that paid me $5k to film for a couple from the Philippians.

Mr. Edgar and Anna were such a loving couple. They were in their early to mid-50s and wanted to renew their vows. Their children were grown and finishing school. She was asked if she wanted to take 40 people on a cruise, all expenses paid, get a four-karat ring upgrade to the already loaded ring she was wearing, or have a wedding, and she chose the wedding.

This wedding was a Catholic wedding and would be the first and last one I would film. I loved the people, but the wedding ceremony was very different for me. They exchanged coins, which was new to me but normal. The rings were something I knew, and I was cool, but then they went to a statue and prayed for a long while, and that made my eyes go around the church.

I felt this weird feeling like eyes were on me, and I couldn't shake the feeling. Needless to say, not my cup of tea. I filmed that from a distance. But besides the church, everything went without a hitch–

except the photographer sucked!

I filmed everything well, but her pictures were garbage. I offered to compensate them for her services, and during the vent, I found a way to produce pictures and whipped out my backup to ensure the event was successful. Funny note: I hired the guy who hired me to work a few jobs for his company on weddings.

It was not to be the boss over my old boss. Not about telling him what to do, but when you can see your growth and obtain mutual respect, it is humbling and an awesome feeling. I withheld part of the photographer's money and gave it to the client for the craziness.

They got my video and loved it so much they said, "We could have just done the video, honestly. You did a great job. Keep the rest as a tip!" So, again, it was a good experience for me to be in business.

My final job with my company was for $10k. I didn't know if this job was really in my lap. I got a call one day from a woman who asked if I was a production company and to give her a quote for filming an event at a hotel for three days.

I told her I would email her a quote, but I didn't get anything back from her. Like a month went by, and I got a call. On the other end was the boss of the lady who called me before, and she said,

From a Drizzle to Light Rain

"Hey, I understand you are our production company for..." a large company. I didn't even know I got the contract, so I was not prepared for the job at the moment–but how many of ya'll know I got ready on the call?

"Yes, I am." "Great, I will email you the details and meet you for the walk-through." We hung up, and I called the school. My other jobs were easy and straightforward, but this was at the Ritz Carlton. I had to get general liability insurance, find two more camera personnel, and manage the shoot to ensure we missed nothing.

The client didn't want us to edit the footage, only film it. I couldn't be a videographer on this job because I needed to manage the event. The guy who got the internship with me at the station, I hired for this event and a few of the graduated students. I even hired my teacher!

I didn't want them to be underwhelmed by my stature and youthful face. I was eighteen at the time, and when I met the Corporate Coordinator, they thought my teacher owned the company. It was funny to see him point me out as the owner! I hired three guys who had families and paid them more than fair. I kept the rest and it was a good day for me too!

I loved working for myself, and I wanted to keep doing it. I was seeing the blessing, the increase, from the works of my hands, and I felt empowered.

If you ever need a confidence boost, reflect on the things you have achieved. When you get scared about moving forward, lean on your accomplishments. Remember what you achieved when you were scared, felt ill-prepared, or unqualified for.

Just something else that came to me, when I got a job as a stagehand working to setup the video elements for this same large hotel and others. That experience for managing that job landed me a managerial position. I had friends like Gunner and Steve, who I called Sticks because he was an incredible drummer.

It was funny, I know, to see this little black girl hanging out with these buff white guys wearing long ponytails. To manage them was icing on the cake! Nobody believed at first I was in charge until three of the guys told them I was. I have been blessed and gifted to do everything I wanted to try.

I even joined a rock band for a bit. Actually, twice, I joined a group. I also joined a pop group once that was looking to work with a large music exec in Orlando. I bowed out; it wasn't what I wanted, and my stepfather was a hater then, too. I always got picked for acting stuff, modeling, and things like that, but it was eerie being in that business. I happily settled into Corporate America.

Back to the shoot. I felt a slue of emotions when I took on this job. During the shoot, it felt good to be the manager. Smile. I didn't mind supporting the vision of others and have always been a team player.

It was nice, though, to be responsible for paying people and ensuring the client was happy. Customer service has always been a big deal for me. However, individuals and corporations were two different things.

It was nice to see my elevation in this way. You will also notice when you shift from individuals to businesses, the demands are different. The expectations can be higher, and the pressure may be more taxing. Sometimes, the pressure of high stakes or more than two pairs of eyes on your work at a time can make you nervous. Don't allow the nerves to hold you back from taking bigger jobs that will stretch your abilities and encourage your faith.

Walking around the floor and going from room to room to check on the guys was work I enjoyed. I liked making the plans and keeping the schedule. Going back to my talents, I always liked to help people.

Sometimes, the basic interpretations of our talents may feel small. For example, I like to help people. Helping people could be assisting an elderly person across the street. Doing dishes, taking out the trash, or giving a compliment to someone.

Helping people can also include building systems, seeing them as a patient, and providing coaching or counseling services. As you see your gifts blossom and mature to match your purpose, allow your growth to happen with it. We are not born knowing everything. I am sure that in each of my jobs, I had something I learned to do better. The client might not have complained, but I learned something in business and about myself each time.

I encourage you to do a checklist and see what you can improve on each time you reach a milestone. Although I wanted to keep this entrepreneurial spirit going because I believed in myself, an economic crisis was brewing. Sometimes we are on fire but the timing to be fully released is not yet.

The clouds can be moving into position to release what looks to be rain, and the gray sky hovers over. The clouds are giving you the signs. You can see the transformation, the change, the progress, and what you desire is within reach, right?

Yet something seems to keep it further off than your grasp. Yet, we still must press on and not lose faith.

Chapter 5

Scripture from Deuteronomy 24:19

I had a thirst to work for myself. My fire and passion for self-employment was there, but my life was not just my own. I was married, and we had to make a joint decision. Have you ever felt like moving with someone else blocked a decision you could have made? If I were to take a job, it felt like a piece of me was dying because my business was stalling. I was offered a full time position with the station and everyone told me to take it; but a part of me didn't want to accept it.

We say we will keep up with everything, but the chances of pulling that off was not realistic with school and everything else I had going on. It was a difficult time for me internally and I had no one to turn to. Everyone thought the job offer was a sweet deal, but I saw it as bondage or giving up something

I wanted for what everyone else wanted for me.

I couldn't go against my husband, so I knew his say would lead the way to the right decision. My husband was level-headed and a good planner. He was also gifted in speaking and connecting with people.

He made me fall in love with his heart for helping people and doing what was right to spread the Gospel. I know things have changed for him personally over the years, but I pray the speaker in him and the heart he has for people can live through him still. When you see a good talent, it is hard to unsee it even if you are not around to see it.

I will always argue that obedience is greater than sacrifice. A Bible verse the Lord tells us to regard. He wants us to be obedient to His voice and calling more than we are willing to give up things, sacrifice, or struggle. You can sacrifice your car, but if He didn't ask for it, you are just suffering.

Many of us give away what we need to survive, and we call that virtue. However, when the good Lord provides, He expects us to be good stewards. How can you be a good steward if you give everything away and have nothing for yourself?

A famous analogy that never gets old. If you're on a plane, they tell you to put on your own mask first before someone else's. This is so you essentially don't die saving someone else.

The Gray Cloud Hovers

Then why do we feel guilty when we do what is best for ourselves? Now, this isn't what I am referencing about the job, but the opposite. I could have turned down the position and did what I wanted to do, but would Yah have been pleased with me?

Would it have been the Father's will for me to reject the advice of my husband to do me? Especially if that means causing discord between him and me, weakening our new marriage? I knew that as a wife, my mission was to surrender to my husband.

It doesn't mean he is going to always make the right choice. He won't. He can make mistakes. I can make them, too. So what we agreed to do, was to come together and talk things out, and if we couldn't agree, we would pray on it.

Sometimes, people say they are scared to do that. To put the final say to prayer. I want to ask, do you think people are afraid to follow that rule because they won't get an answer?

Follow-up question: Do you think God is a mute? That He doesn't hear and cannot speak? That if you pray, it will fall on deaf ears?

Or is it that people think God is powerless? We say He is all-powerful in our prayers. We say He is the foundation of our marriage and our faith, but do we practice that when we are tested? My husband and I prayed, but the decision he made was the same. Every time we disagreed, it didn't go his way, but on this occasion, it did.

I wasn't mad, but I was sad for a bit because accepting this position meant closing my doors. The same faith I had that the decision my husband made would work for our good. I needed to believe that if He did it before, He would do it again! I needed to be reminded that as the rain might appear to not drip at all, maybe my heart was wrong and not the choice.

I stopped praying for God to change my husband but for Him to change my heart. When we learn to pray prayers that we need, and not for others only, we can receive the healing we need also. Have you found that it is easy to put everyone else's prayers before your own?

Are you quick to list the things the family needs, but slow to tell the Father what you need? How you feel? Can you tell the Father your deep feelings and expose your vulnerability, humanity, and need for him to save you? Or do you present your pain and leak anger and resentment–and almost come off as judging instead of loving?

I had to check my heart to be in right position for the rain. And how many of you know that when we are obedient, God will honor us in private and before men? I took the job, and at the early onset, I was still able to complete my old task. I liked being on golf courses and helping with live productions.

It was nothing like the quiet on a course with

good weather that welcomed the scenery. It made my heart light, and I enjoyed cruising on the golf court to run whatever they needed back and forth. It gave me a chance to get away from a desk, a cubical, to enjoy the sun and fresh air.

I was free in my position and had sick days and time off. I still was me and could be free on a day if I needed it. Crazy to think this freelance position could turn salaried, and I could participate in activities that meant I left work for two hours two to three days a week! I was in love with working at the station. I enjoyed the responsibility and the gift of having a job without the degree required.

I was about 20 when I got paid 33k to start a position requiring a bachelor's. To have my position, I needed a bachelor's degree. I had an associates and a technical certificate that this job had already helped me get faster. I was fully employed before finishing school. I completed my program with zero debt but a surplus!

After working for a few months, I got a raise and was near 37k. They offered to pay for some of my school if I agreed to stay with them for five years. Funny, I didn't need the money.

I went for free because I had scholarship money and financial aid left. I worked my shift and they gave me the time off I needed to study when exams came up. I had two years left to finish my bachelor's.

I still got a *Kiss From Yah*. Don't you just love this book title? I dedicated poems to the Father and His children because this is one of the sweetest ways I could express the feeling you get from being His child. It is the little things that make you so grateful and mindful of Him in your everyday life. If you like poetry and shorts, it is a page-turner; cheers!

Right, back at it. I was rewarded for believing and being obedient even through my discomfort. Choosing to take this position was one of the best things that happened to me. I got health insurance, a 401k, and I learned a lot. Everyone in my department was older than me by seven to over ten years. The wealth of information I got in a simple everyday chat taught me how to move in a corporate setting.

I was respectful, but I learned what corporate demands, and I began to rise to the occasion. I worked this job, and so many people took me under their wing to help me learn how to deal with clients. I had never talked to an executive anywhere until this position. To jump in and call large car companies' ad agencies and meet a pro base baller turned voice-over talent was humbling. He always had great things to share and was a sweet guy.

I saw his ring for winning a world series, and it was amazing! Who knew I would be telling him what to say and leading the audio session in my early twenties? I knew not everyone was happy for me, but I paid that no mind. I felt if I was going to have haters, glad they were above me.

The Gray Cloud Hovers

When they are above you, your failing is them failing as it relates to management. I remember when I got this position, the lady who trained me told me what to do one time. I had never seen the documents before or knew how to find where to save and submit files. She was very brief and curt. She didn't want to answer any of my questions without rolling her eyes or breathing funny like I was bothering her.

I wasn't sure what it was about me that bothered her, but I wasn't going to let her push me out of anything. I did my best, and in the beginning, I made so many small mistakes. I made mistakes for about two weeks, and I thought I was going to get fired.

I remember praying and asking Yah, "Why would you give me a job that is too hard for me? You said you wouldn't put more on me than I can bear." I felt like a failure because of the simple mistakes that kept creeping up in my work.

I came in early and stayed late all the time. I sometimes worked through my lunches, and my efforts were seen by the boss over my boss and the whole department. Mrs. Laura called me into her office and said, "Krystal. How are things going?"

I replied, "They are not going too well. I apologize for the many small mistakes. I am trying to go back over my notes and see if I missed anything each time."

"So, how much training did you get?"

"She showed me how to do everything one time."

"Really?"

"Yes, ma'am."

"Well, that is not enough for anybody to learn this position. I am impressed you have been able to retain anything with such little training. I am going to give you two weeks of training that you should have had already."

"Oh, thank you so much, Mrs. Laura." A conversation that should have been for my firing turned into a promotion. I thought the rain was hiding or that something was wrong. Turned out God was just holding an umbrella to shield me from the storm. He took a low point in my life and turned it into a moment for me to lean on His love. He carried me through.

The woman who didn't want to talk to me was much nicer this time around. She didn't have to train me for two weeks. In a week I got it, and I had nearly no errors after that. I was catching errors the clients were making. I didn't feel good to see anyone make mistakes, but it felt good for mistakes not to be mine so often.

I did so well in my position that I got two

raises in the first year I worked for the station. I was happy, and there were no more talks of concern about my position. My immediate manager never knew enough details about my training. The lady who trained me told him it was done, and I didn't know to tell the difference.

He helped teach me other editing techniques that I still use today. I learned to edit in video production school. However, doing it at a professional level, my immediate report manager taught me that. Things at the station were going well until they got bought out by another company. This station was determined to change a lot of things and cut costs.

The first line of people to enter the unemployment line were people who had twenty years or more at the company. It was sad to see these really proficient managers leave. I knew that nothing would last forever, and the way these managers were leaving the company was full of grace. Some were even excited about their severance packages and making plans on what to do with their retirement.

That financial bubble that had been building for a decade was about to erupt and stop the world– or at least American homeowners in their tracks. Many of the people who got their tickets and severance were about to walk into a recession, but the Father still made provision through the rain! This recession was a messy one when the housing bubble burst.

I was not a homeowner at the time; we were still getting things together. I was pregnant and near delivery when the layoffs started taking place. I wanted to be there for my daughter, so my job became less important as my due date grew closer. I was the pregnant lady who refused to stop working and worked until the day I would give birth.

People kept asking me about my plans for after my baby was born, and I kept saying to be a great mom and manage my responsibilities. I remember the other four black people who worked at the station told me in code, whatever you choose to do, don't say nothing. Just do it.

In my position, I got maternity leave, so I would have six weeks off. I didn't want to start my six weeks if I had to go back to work a day earlier than when I landed in the hospital. I went into the hospital on Labor Day, a Monday, so it was paid. I laughed about that all the time that I went into labor on Labor Day 2009. She was due in another two weeks, but she wanted out at 38 weeks, and I was cool with that.

Meanwhile, my husband was overseas for the war while I was in the hospital. It was a busy time for both of us. He wanted me to return after I gave birth, but I wanted to be home with our daughter. I couldn't see myself giving up my new baby for someone else to raise. I wanted to be there to breastfeed and see what she needed.

The Gray Cloud Hovers

Again, I started to feel that familiar feeling for when I released my production company. But this isn't a business baby; this is my baby. My husband and I didn't agree, and we resorted to asking God what to do next. During this prayer, I remember having a peace about everything. I remained calm and focused on enjoying my baby.

We had a few more conversations, and he tried to plead that I needed to work because the recession was coming, and we needed to store and save. I told him that some things were more important. He thought I was crazy and unrealistic, and I understood why. But I kept praying because that was important for me.

At the job, positions were being absorbed, and management and new hires were being cut next. I was in my position for about two or three years when things shook up. I remember it was a regular day, and my phone rang. It was the station and I wasn't sure if they needed something from me. I was asked to come in, and my sister watched the baby for me.

I went to the office, and there was a new manager who I found out replaced Mrs Laura. They told me not to be alarmed. Everything is fine, but they are making some changes and looking at how to consolidate our department. They are looking at everyone, and they wanted to give me a heads-up. I said I understood, and then they asked, "If we were to offer you a severance package of this amount, you can apply for unemployment in a few weeks. Would you take it?"

Without hesitation, I said, "Yes." They gave me several months' pay. I could keep my insurance plan for 6 months, file for unemployment, finish out my maternity leave, and combine my holiday, sick days, and time earned. I was leaving that office, grinning from ear to ear.

I heard what other people got for leaving and the many who were let go with no severance. I was leaving with everything I needed and some. My husband wasn't mad, but he stressed that I had better have what I needed because I had let the job go. Do you know that the Father provided for me to be unemployed for an entire year? The government kept extending tier benefits to the millions of people who couldn't get a job.

I was blessed beyond measure!

The Father Sends the Rain

Scripture from Amos 4:7

During the recession, most of us were stuck between a rock and a hard place. But it was like Amos 4:7 in my world.

"I also withheld the rain from you when there were yet three months to the harvest; I would send rain on one city and send no rain on another city; one field would have rain, and the field on which it did not rain would wither..."

I literally saw many of us who were let go with severance doing better and less stressed than when working the job! We were all happier and found that it was raining on us in a famine.

It was raining on us, even though it wasn't raining on the person next to me. The lady who trained me absorbed my position into her recently acquired position. Editors who worked there were cut down from five to two. There were two audio engineers, but at the end, it was only one. Those who were my friends were all blessed.

I remember one was happily married to a judge. He celebrated her achievements all the time. It was a great example for me to see a power melinated couple doing it big in my eyes. He said when he retired, he was going to spend more time with her, and they were going to continue to grow old together. He also told me, "Don't waste all your years chasing other people's dreams. Find your own, and build something."

Another was able to switch his position and go on and work for another station in a different state. He was great at what he did and had been with the company for over a decade. We still stay in touch, and his baby girl, who was two years old when he moved, is now an adult.

Wow, how time moves, right? He had no problem with getting employment. Another was able to stay and kept working on the productions he loved. It was great to see others move on to work for shopping networks, move to LA, and the list went on and on.

The lady who had twice as much work to do earned the same pay. Crazy sometimes how double for your trouble can literally be double trouble.

The Father Sends the Rain

When times are hard, you are even grateful for the struggle. I think they were surprised to see how pleased I was, because others were panicking to hear the news. I didn't miss one moment of my daughter's life, and she stayed with me until she was able to speak full sentences at nearly two years old, which was my prayer.

The only bad feeling I had at this time was that I missed out on turning in my final writing assignment to get my minor in writing. I had the grades and the electives to earn it. I remember when I talked to our department dean and he told me, "Do you know the material?"

I replied, "Yes."

He said, "Then the rest is just paper. Go be with your family and stop stressing." I was working on my bachelor's degree while I was pregnant. I was due to give birth at the end of the semester when my finals were due. I turned everything in early because I didn't want to fail.

I could no longer be disappointed because the assignment was done. Looking at my daughter's face put things back into perspective for me. Sometimes, the rain stops because life has a way of introducing new life. The rain could be about money, it could be about family, or it could be about joy.

On this day, I felt the rain and the sun pop out to paint a Florida picturesque scene. Some may say, how can you be happy to have children when you are so young and starting your career? But for me, children will always be a priority. I can always get more money, but I cannot get back time.

Faith carried me, and new options opened up daily to get me where I needed to be. I was planning even though I felt like life was standing still. I got on WIC and any other program I could find.

I took family planning courses to get diapers and baby clothes. I went to food pantries to try and stretch what I had. I didn't have to pay the mortgage on the house because my husband paid for it. He bought the house only in his name, so I wasn't liable for the house, and technically, I didn't own it.

I had all the other bills, and unemployment gave me $1,200 a month. So, my car note, insurance, food, health, and anything our daughter needed, I got it for her. I was buying stuff with no money, and my sister would say that it wasn't fair. "You shouldn't have to live like this, Krystal." If I had a bill that was over the norm or unexpected, my husband would say he wasn't paying for the difference and to go get a job.

I knew it was his way of encouraging me to carry my load. Eventually, I got a job at a church I respected and worked as a teacher. I had a degree, so I got more than the other teachers who didn't. I picked this job because I wanted to still be close to our daughter in case there was an issue.

The Father Sends the Rain

I couldn't be her teacher, but I was down the hall and would see her at recess sometimes. It was so cute to see her in her world. I didn't want to bother her, but I watched from afar. What mothers do for their children is admirable. What women who have a *Mothering Spirit* would do for children is the same.

I wrote the book *Mothering Spirit* because no one can truly understand the responsibility mothers feel unless they are given the job of caring for children. I think it is unfortunate when people who don't like or love children are entrusted with their wellbeing. I don't believe you have to have children to be a mother, but you do have to have a love for children. It is a special mandate on a woman's life that bubbles from the inside and begs for a child to share it with.

If you want children and it hasn't happened, hang on. If you have children and you are growing through mistakes, don't give up. If you have lost children, it does get better, and you still have more to give even when you think you don't. You don't have to birth children to have a mothering heart. I share more in the book; pick it up and be encouraged.

Let's bring it back. I enjoyed teaching the little 2-year-olds. I had a class of about four children when I started. I was in the overflow class. The other class had about ten children in it, so quickly, they decided to merge our classes since enrollment started to die down. I grew close to my first four, but it was nice to have fourteen babies!

I enjoyed pushing the wagon and having children from every background. I have stories that will stay in my heart forever. I remember I had this child in my Sunday morning class. When we first met, he was very standoffish. He would take toys from other children. Push people, and he wasn't polite to say "please" or "thank you."

He came to my class twice before there was a complete change in him. I would tell him firm but not rude, "You can't push people. If you push people, you won't have a lot of friends that way." He would ignore me and stump off. When other children would help me clean, he would go and try to snatch things out of their hands. "Hey, you can't do that. If you want to help, you can, and I would appreciate your help."

He walked off and folded his hands. I said, "When you're ready to help, I will be here." He didn't storm off that time, and he looked at me with his head tilted sideways. He then started picking up the toys off the floor! I didn't ask him to do it all. When it was time for snack, he said, "Can I help?" I replied, "Of course you can. Thank you so much."

He sat in his chair and was so sweet. He asked for me when he came back the following week, and I smiled at his parents as they left for service. He came in and started playing with the other children. He had a perfect day. He wanted to clean with me even when church was over, and his parents were at the door. He asked them to wait a minute because he wasn't done yet.

The parents asked me, "Does he always do this?"

I said, "He is my little helper," as I smiled at him. He really was a sweet boy.

They looked like they were in shock. The husband said, "He is not like this at home." I didn't say anything but nodded my head and said, "Hmm." Then the mother said, "What did you do? I replied, "I just talked to him. I didn't ask him to help me clean. He wants to do it and is the first one to come and grab a rag." Sometimes, we don't see the rain because our expectations are too low.

You could tell he was used to people doing everything for him. He was brilliant, and I knew he was. I figured he might not be social because he was an only child. So it was normal for children with no siblings to behave differently until they got used to more children. He stayed with me all term. He started giving me hugs when he was leaving for home, and I grew to love him.

The same is true for all my students. I loved each of them, and it was hard for me to see them elevate and go to the next class. I was crying and very emotional about the graduation, and I knew teaching wasn't for me, although I love babies. I was invested, and seeing them leave made me feel like a piece of my heart was going with them.

Working at the church, I made $10 an hour. I took a step back financially, but my soul was happy. I was able to learn new things. I took up sewing classes in my downtime. I could take my daughter to the park and have fun with her. My husband worked overseas our entire marriage. I saw him a few months in a year, and he was gone for the rest of the year.

When I left the church, I picked up another regular job. I went into upholstery! I know, can you imagine my little self working with furniture? I was pulling out staples from chairs, wrapping boat seats with vinyl, and learning how to stretch material.

I had no experience when I got this position. They took me on as an apprentice. When I was learning how to sew at Joanne's with the ladies' group, which met a few days a week, I picked up enough skills to get a job.

I thought I would continue down this path, but the Father had other plans. If I am honest, I was getting comfortable with doing manual labor. I worked hard, so laboring with my hands didn't bother me. I bought machines and got a second position, but this time, I was working for myself, sewing banners for a commercial company. One thing about me: I never saw a drought or light rain as wasted time.

No matter where I was or how things were going, I was determined to make lemonade out of lemons. My attitude was the sugar I needed to make

The Father Sends the Rain

it happen. But I need the water, the increase on what I made to see a harvest. You can have everything set up, but if the Father doesn't send you support, it's just work. We need to rely upon the Lord to show us how to make good use of our time.

The Father is the Great Bridegroom or Farmer. In the Bible, there are many examples of how He compares believers to those who are married and those who are farming. Have you ever wondered why? How many of us, if we knew everything we would have to endure before we got married, would still choose to be married?

Some of us would say, although I love my spouse, marriage is hard. Some wouldn't want to do it again. If women knew what labor pains were like before getting pregnant, how many would be slower to want children? Put another way, if you had no drugs, how many would want them at all?

I am just kidding. I love the verse that says women quickly forget about their labor when they see their child (John 16:21). This is what happens when we experience a relationship that leads to peace and strength.

Nobody minds hearing about the blessing and the gift, but we all would want to skip the pain. What I think is pretty interesting is that pain can be used to do two things. Make you love God more or curse Him.

Believers, we have a word in our mouths like the one found in Job 13:15. Though you slay me; still I will trust you. Or like Paul when he says, I am a bond servant of Christ (Romans 1:1). This means slave not prettied up.

As children of God, we are committed to following Him no matter where he leads us. The good part is that He is wherever we need Him to be–and where He wants to be. No matter where His children go, we cannot escape His Spirit.

Psalm 139 verses 7 through 12 writes:

> *Where shall I go from your Spirit? Or where shall I flee from your presence? 8 If I ascend to heaven, you are there! If I make my bed in Sheol, you are there! 9 If I take the wings of the morning and dwell in the uttermost parts of the sea, 10 even there your hand shall lead me, and your right hand shall hold me. 11 If I say, "Surely the darkness shall cover me, and the light about me be night," 12 even the darkness is not dark to you; the night is bright as the day, for darkness is as light with you.*

What deep depth can we ascend or descend that He is not there? When we are depressed, happy, or indifferent, His Spirit can renew us. He can see us in the dark, and the shadows don't scare Him.

He is not afraid of the secrets we keep or the pain we mask. He is here, and for many of us, in the same place, He said He wanted you to be. But where did you go?

If we use our pain to curse God, we have walked away. We stopped believing in Him and His ability to bless us. We lean on our own understanding and expect the works of our hands to do all that we need.

We pray for the impossible and believe for that, but the day to day, we think I won't trouble Yah. It might sound good, but it is not what He wants. I pray about simple things like parking spaces, what trip to take home, and virtually anything I am led to take for granted.

Do you know when the Towers fell in New York, there were many who were glad when they prayed. The Father told them to take another route, and they did. How glad they were to avoid the disaster.

People who prayed about going to work who called out sick. Those who would have normally been somewhere else on that day were where someone in help needed them to be. There are many stories of how the Father will send us lifelines if only we would listen for Him.

If we allow Him to heal our hearts, maybe pain won't manifest elsewhere. If we watch our mouths, maybe death won't follow us. If we kept the faith in good and difficult times, maybe in marriage, life, finances, business, or career, we could see the beauty in the struggle. The Father knows how to make our crooked paths straight (Isaiah 45:2).

When it was raining in my life, the rain kept piling on. I was transitioned from my salaried position. Then, I went into a lower-paying position. I was feeling scared that I might not have what it takes to compete like before. I was a mother with less time, and being home while my husband made six figures, I felt less than when we talked. He wanted me to get out there and compete with what he could do, but my emotional state wasn't there.

He wanted a successful wife who could put up the same numbers as him, and lately, for the past two years, I wasn't. I was shrinking back and using the time to learn and not earn so much. But was it a strategy or fear?

Scripture from Matthew 9:37-38

If it is not raining on your side, do you keep standing there? If the rain is not refreshing but hitting you with water drops, hail in the size of peas, how can you appreciate the rain? When you are hurting, compliments can feel like hail. People may say, wow, you look nice today. Your response was, "No, I don't. I just put this on and walked out the door."

During this time, I got braces. I was in my twenties, correcting my teeth. I didn't mind it a whole lot, but I felt out of sorts sometimes. I didn't feel like "metal face," but sometimes, when my hair wasn't cooperating with the braces, I just felt like a mess. I stopped relaxing my hair when I got pregnant. So, going natural was a huge change from the flowing, straight hair I had when I met my husband.

I had a look everyone wanted me to have. I would constantly hear you look so much better with your hair straightened. So, for years, I did what was killing my hair; added heat.

Even when you think it is safe, it still causes some damage. My hair could take heat, but still, I liked my hair to dance up to the sun–but my husband didn't. It wasn't personal to me; it was just his preference. To be fair, he didn't meet me that way.

When I got compliments for my natural hair, I thought people were lying or trying to talk to me, so I ignored it. I didn't think I was pretty. I had a baby I was raising alone, I had no career, my hair was nappy, and I had braces. I wasn't shiny like a penny. I was twenty-three, but I knew I wasn't eighteen or twenty anymore. Life for me had changed, and things were changing for both of us.

If I was honest, we were never fully on the same page. He wanted to rent an apartment for the first few years of our marriage. He was nervous when we found out we were pregnant. I was excited and saw a reason to move to a larger place and buy.

For a year, I looked for the right house. I went and saw at least a hundred houses, I feel. They were selling fast during the boom. As the market started to correct, prices were getting in range.

When our daughter was first born, I took her home to our two-bedroom apartment. I was okay

Work Through The Rain

with being there in the beginning. My sister stayed with me in the extra room, so she kept me company while my husband was out of the country.

I didn't want to sit around during my time off, even if I was getting paid to be there. I started my master's program online at Liberty University. I always wanted to study to show myself approved, and when I could get a Master's in a theological study, I didn't hesitate to enroll.

You know how the Father does. He showed me a way to attend debt-free! This time, the military paid for my program because I was a spouse of an active service member. I would be breastfeeding and reading books, typing papers, and responding to posts on Blackboard.

I don't know if I would have had the time to commit to school if I had had a real job during this time. My schedule was busy, and even with my sister around, I had less and less time to care for my dog. I was heartbroken when I had to rehome her. My Maggy will always be precious to me.

One thing I hated that my husband wanted to do was get a bark collar. I didn't know how the thing worked. I just knew it went on like a normal collar and had a round attachment that looked like a batter, I guessed. I didn't realize that the collar actually shocks the dog when they bark to train them to stop.

I am not sure if it was my fault or what was

wrong, but it was burning the fur and skin off my dog! The arguments that took place about her eventually left me in silence. I knew keeping her was not going to work, and now, I barely had time to go downstairs to walk her three times a day like we used to.

So I searched for a good person who I felt would take care of her and honestly want her and not breed her. I found a thirteen-year-old girl who said her mom wouldn't let her get a puppy, but a dog that was already potty trained. Maggy was about three, so she was good at that. I knew she would be happy, even if I was sad for a while.

I think I was a little depressed when I married because so many things were changing about me. What I wanted out of life, what I believed I could do, and what I was worth. Even though I had degrees, had made decent money, and wasn't ugly, at the moment, none of those things mattered.

I could only see what I thought was my reality. I wasn't good enough, and the only person who wanted me was the same one who needed me, Kayda. She made me smile so many times when I just wanted to cry.

Even though I had respected my husband's choices, I started to feel bad that if I had made my own choice to keep my company, could I have been poor now? It made me think maybe my choices would have led me wrong. I was spiraling a bit, but I had no one to turn to. My mom's marriage was holding on by a string most days. None of my siblings were married, and my extended family wasn't close.

So, I did what I thought was best and just stayed busy. I learned sewing, as I said, too. It was funny to see me go into Joannes with my car seat, and Kayda would sleep through the whole class.

People thought she was a toy sometimes because she never cried. She was an easy baby and could sleep fine. I had no reason to complain, so I didn't. But I should have talked more.

When I was in pre-marital counseling, she suggested I wait to get married. I expressed waiting, but then he made up his mind to get married. We were just frequently on different wavelengths, so when the marriage ended, we, too, couldn't agree. It was hard to see where I had come down to–arguable, one could say.

I needed a mist something to help me push along. Life took yet a turn again when I felt I needed to start on a different path. I've always thought of being an entrepreneur, so I got into sewing. I feel like knowing the basics can go a long way, so I started to learn how to sew. To learn how to sew, I bought machines that could make my job easier. I plan to make money from anything I spend money on.

So, if it is not making money, it is just a liability. The money I spend on my children is an investment in their joy and future. I pray someday they will appreciate me if all goes well. I give my life to make sure they have one because my legacy is also in them. But really for the Kingdom at large, because whoever I touch, I pray that becomes part of my legacy too. Your legacy can extend far beyond your family.

Everything I have ever done has always been for the benefit of more people than just myself. Yes, when I was a child, I wanted a fashion line, and this was a great time to work it out. Only I didn't know how to sew. So what do I do? I jumped into the sewing classes, learned enough, and started a business.

I took the machine I had and started looking for jobs on Craigslist. Something that was a hobby turned into a business idea for me. I have always loved quilting. I remember it was an art for my ancestors during slavery, so I wanted to learn. I always had a love for history and culture.

I learned to quilt, and I wasn't the best, but I learned to stitch and sew. I got an embroidery machine. I loved that thing. Cost me a few thousand dollars. My husband thought I was crazy. But I got it. I expanded and started looking for a job with the machines. I started at an interview and passed the test. I had to sew before an audience. I wasn't super fast, but I was precise.

They told me to sew a banner, and after they saw it, they said I had the job. I knew my machine was going to be slow with vinyl, so I needed a better machine if I kept going. Good thing I kept making money, and I loved what I did. The company used the banners to hang up in housing subdivisions.

I kept banging out those banners until I left Florida for Georgia. When the housing complexes slowed down for a bit, but they soon ramped up again when I was preparing to leave. It was great to make money doing something I loved. My husband, however, thought I needed to look for better work. He thought manual labor was beneath my potential.

I wasn't the best, but I managed to do what they asked of me. I knew my personal life was changing, and I was falling into a production mindset of being content with being a worker using my hands. I did lose sight of what was in front of me, like a fog hovering over a lake. I didn't see the future anymore, and I was okay with what I had. That fire within me was dying, so I knew I needed to change course. My marriage was dying, and one day, it broke.

When it did, I moved in search of a future. I got to Georgia, and the air felt cool, blowing on me. I knew this was a place I needed to be. I wasn't sure of what I would do here, but I wanted to see.

I looked for jobs but leaned on the last thing I was doing. I moved with two industrial sewing machines, one embroidery machine, a serger, and my original sewing machine. I loved what I did and was committed. I had tons of fabric and was going to go into window treatments and embroidery.

I needed more strength, if I was honest, because the material was heavy, and guiding it was harder. It seemed like the water had stopped, but the sky was still gray. I thought maybe I had mistaken the road I was to travel and gave into the attempt to return to a marriage already broken.

The make-up was brief, and I left again within a month, this time for good. I couldn't go to the home. It felt strange, like a cage or a coffin I died in already. I had been revived, and I wanted to stay that way.

I moved back to Georgia again, but I had to be honest in our final conversation. Man, it was painful and scary. I was convicted to be with him like I was living in sin or something.

I knew it was the wrong connection we had now. Something was different, and I guess, in part, the difference was me. I knew then that whatever we had was confirmed dead, and I had to move on.

I never gave up on life, but what was the goal changed. When we were going through the divorce, he was in and out of the country. I didn't want to stay in Florida anymore. It just brought out pain to me.

It was cold although it was sunny. My heart wasn't fuzzy; It was freezing. So that's why I decided to move and stay in Georgia.

When I came to the Peach State, my brother was so kind as to allow me to stay with him, and I was grateful. I knew I couldn't stay long, and I needed to get on my feet. I applied to jobs, but I was intimidated to apply for anything concrete.

I didn't know what the block was. I only knew I could use my hands, and I was scared to use my mind. I invested in my education but was not ready to use it, I guess.

I ended up landing jobs for sewing. But I wasn't that good at working for high-paced companies. I was too slow, so they let me go. It was strange to be fired for the first time. It was just bad timing, I guess. I knew I had to be different, and I couldn't fail. My daughter needed me to survive, and I had to prove I could take care of her for the custody part of the divorce.

I had hardly any money because I didn't save much, and I worked jobs that paid barely enough. I pawned my wedding ring and got nothing for it. That paid for gas. I applied for a position at a Christian media agency on a whim through an online application site. This was the first job I tried and wanted to get. I love God, and this seemed like the right move.

I wasn't nervous about the interview because I knew whatever will be, will be. Funny, I never stopped studying the Bible and pursuing God while the storm was raging around me. I learned to accept the storm but not allow it to move me no more. I stopped worrying about what I looked like and changed my hairstyle to something I liked. I even got a little color in it, so I was feeling like my old self and my mom said I looked like my old self, too.

Either the same day or the next day, I got a call from that company. They said after reviewing the candidates, they were prepared to offer any of the following three positions: writer, executive assistant, or sales. Can you imagine? All this time, I couldn't get one job, and then in one interview, I was offered three different positions!

I felt the cloud roll back earlier in my heart, but now it was manifesting in my natural life. I was able to dig myself out of the mud. I bought a house I had looked at a few weeks prior on faith. I bout a 70k house with 5k down owner financed. She gave me a year to finance the house for the balance.

I had my second salaried position, making almost double, and I could move out into my own house as soon as I finished repairs. The house wasn't perfect, but it had the structure to become three times what I paid for it if I could get the renovations done. I was doing better until I lost focus.

When we are on our A game, the enemy will throw us curve balls that are meant for us to stop what we are doing to catch it. Not necessarily to dismiss your future but to have you delay it. I believe I

Work Through The Rain

could have paid off that house and moved into it if I didn't get sidetracked with a relationship that would go nowhere for 6 years.

It sucked my time, a lot of it in the beginning, then in the later years, it was a boomerang that I needed to break in half. Eventually, that was what I did, but the damage had already been done. Now, we are back, and I have two girls. I worked this job for a year, and I was good at what I did, and I loved it. I loved the people and the company. The job was a bit awkward because the owner could get upset and fire you in a meeting on the spot.

I remember I disagreed with him about something, and I was dismissed. Funny thing, I felt no sting when it happened. I was looking out for his best interest and that of the client, so if I was fired for that, I was okay. I politely gathered my things and told everyone thank you for the opportunity, and left.

I got a call about an hour and a half later from the business. I thought I had left something behind, so I answered to see what it was. I was asked to return to work that same day. I said I would take the day off and come in tomorrow.

It was sweet to leave for an early lunch because I got fired. Extend the break, then get a call to say I was hired back! Whew, look at God!

That's Not Rain, But Hail

Chapter 8

Scripture from Psalm 107:37-38

That happened a few times, so I am glad I have thick skin, and dismissals don't alarm me. I ended up leaving the company but on my own terms. I was hired back on for freelance gigs in the future so it was no harm–just business. In business, you have to learn to walk in your integrity, but don't wear your heart on your sleeve. Bleeding hearts can have you compromise, overwork yourself in a negative way, and you end up empty-handed.

I was there first and left last still many nights. I knew this was my integrity and an example of my commitment. If something needed to be done, it was getting done.

I didn't leave excuses but found a way to fix things and kept going. I learned resilience with this company and fine-tuned problem-solving. I learned from brilliant people, and I realized how much my brain was capable of.

On this job, I was resourceful, and my goal was to work to prove the skill set they already believed I had. I worked with the Creative Director as his executive assistant. My function was to keep him organized and provide him with the details he couldn't fill in because he was editing and producing. I had a production understanding, so scheduling jobs wasn't an issue.

I had a bachelor's in English and scriptwriting experience from school and the station. I was savvy on how to function in a successful corporation and management was a gift I had long before the corporate world. Connecting with people and making sure people were good was my heart always. So, I wanted to ensure the client and our staff were good with projects.

This media agency wasn't serving clients of any industry, per say, but catered to faith-based products and content. We managed well-known pastors' media accounts and assisted them in buying time and selling time on stations. We had strategy meetings with pastors in India, Nigeria, Australia, and the US. It was an incredible experience to see Yah (God) move all around the world at this job.

For us all to be able to speak the same love language of God was truly remarkable. It really

That's Not Rain, But Hail

made me want to work harder, be more committed, and consistent than I was before. I really understood the scripture in Galatians 6:10, which says, "O then, as we have opportunity, let us do good to everyone, and especially to those who are of the household of faith."

Working to combine my love for media, writing, and sales was a great experience and confirmation. Although I loved the job, I saw a shift in how television would work moving forward, and I didn't want my window to close for what I wanted to accomplish. It has always been in my heart to have a media station. When I first desired one, I said tv station, but that is becoming a dinosaur.

We are mostly on our phones, tvs, and streaming apps; rarely does anyone watch standard television. Most people don't watch cable anymore either because of apps they can stream on smart tvs. I saw this when I was working at this media agency. I shared this with the owner in light conversation.

I am sure the media agency space has changed and will continue to be revamped over the years to come. I didn't leave this company on any ill-will. My heart was to be in a position to achieve what I felt I was supposed to do. I am to create content and reach the goal of owning distribution channels. The real money in media is in distribution.

I wanted to control what I was building, so a station, a page, a channel was where my sights shifted to. I didn't have a Facebook page or social page until 2012. I was not joining for personal reasons but to understand the business of social interaction. I wanted a way to connect with people who might not live next door, but our destinies are connected.

My sister set up my account, and I was so nervous about my privacy being breached. Haha, yes, I was one of those people, and I still have reservations about social media. But I embraced the platform a few years later. I had zero posts for like a year or two. Nikki (my sister) was like "Let me help you, Girl." She put up a few posts for me, and then I had a friend of mine help me post to get things going when I started to see what I was going to do in 2016.

It was in 2016 that I decided to write and publish my first book! I was freelancing at the media agency to help with production shoots and when they needed a hand with management on a big project. One project was with an established pastor who wanted to publish another book (he was already a repeat author). The company brought in to speak about publication was a local publishing company. The owners were two women, one a lawyer and the other a writer.

It was a blessing to meet these ladies and learn of their skills and partnership. I asked if Myrna could help me with my book! She said, "No, you can learn to do it yourself." I thought she was joking, but she wasn't. She told me if I got stuck or needed her help, she would be there for me, and she was. We

That's Not Rain, But Hail

can think that if someone helps us, it means they are doing it for us. But the real power is in learning how to do it yourself so you can teach others!

I started the process of writing my first book, Alone But Never Lonely: Katherine. It took me–I thought a long time to write it. I wrote it over a few months, but I was stuck on how to end it. I felt like there wasn't a perfect marker because my life was still going. I did omit many parts of my life to focus on the part relevant to the topic. It was while reviewing my goal for the book that I found the ending to be clear.

You don't have to reveal your entire life story in a book, but share the aspects of your story to help people see how they can overcome. I published that book, and I was so excited to have completed it. I attended a few local events to speak about the book and sold books in person every time. I remember leaving a meeting, and someone asked, "You got a book now?" I replied, "Yes, in the car." He said, "I will buy it before I leave."

I was encouraged that my story could impact people. I was nervous about the mistakes people would find because my process then wasn't as good as it is now. Even now, I am still guilty of minor grammatical infractions. So, if you see one, don't be too hard on me, smile.

I remember one day sitting at my computer, and the Father was teaching me how we can love what we love and pursue it to our detriment. We want the Ecstasy, the highs in life that feel good for a moment, but the end is hell, death.

During this time in my life, things were good for a moment. But how many of you know the rain came? I shifted down, perhaps because I picked a relationship doomed to fail. The house I was working to renovate, I lost. The credit line I got from the bank to fix the house and make repairs was gone. The asset I thought I was building to have a home for my child, I never got to live in.

I was the one who worked to have a house and do the repairs. I never slept a night in it. It was a relief to give the house back because when my savings were running down, I had to transition to focus on what was important. I needed food stamps to feed us. I had no place to live because what I was building was gone. We were homeless!

I stayed with my mother while I was repairing my house. I was on her couch and I slept there when I was pregnant with my second child. The plans he made to help me fix the house never happened. I was able to work my side jobs and make enough to contribute to my mom's house when my job went away.

I didn't believe in staying with a man I wasn't married to, so his house wasn't an option. I would stay the night or stay a few days but always came back to my mom's after. I remember when I was pregnant. He told me to move in with him so we could care for the baby together.

I was considering it, but there was a day when he told me to leave. "Go back to your mother's house since you don't want to stay here." So I left that day holding my tv that I put in the car myself. This was a 50-inch tv. He felt some kind of way after hearing about meetings I had and speaking on the phone to pastors or any man in general.

I rode down the elevator and left out of his Buckhead sky-rise. It was the next day he told me to come back. It was then my choice not to live with him after our child was born was cemented. I didn't trust him, although I wanted to. When my mom lost her place, I got a place in Conyers. I was doing great, and I was stable. My mom then moved in with me!

But I made a mistake that haunted me almost instantly. I tried to work things out with my youngest daughter's dad. He borrowed money from me while he drove a Maserati. I laugh because it makes no sense. I am the one who was "poor," but he comes to me to borrow. He always paid it back, but I never borrowed from him.

I ended up losing that place, my car, and my belief that he would ever change to be with me. However, I still believe the Father can redeem him for himself. For me, he was like an omen of bad change and a "no" the Father wasn't changing.

After all of this happened again, I lost three

properties, one after another, whenever he and I tried to make amends. This time, it clicked. There was nothing to mend. I had to accept this was over and move on.

My daughter was the result of the rain. She brought the sun out and showed me my time spent wasn't a drought. Zoe brought life during and after the rain.

In between losing my house, getting a house, losing it, and getting another, I stayed with both of my sisters. I am thankful I didn't always have a bed to sleep on but the floor because it kept me uncomfortable. I was grateful to have it because it could have been worse. When it rains, and you have a box to sleep under, how grateful are you that the rain doesn't spank your face as it falls?

I wasn't used to begging or being in need. I was the one who gave to them and not the other way around. It was a humbling experience to be displaced a few times in my life. I got my own place eventually, and I started getting things together.

I learned that when your windshield wipers don't work, the last thing you need is rain. I wasn't ready for the downpour that started because of my lack of obedience. So I prayed for shelter from the rain and to never return to where I escaped out of the mouth of the dragon. I hid from the rain instead of embracing it. I needed to be renewed, and as I committed to that growth, I saw the Father moving in my life again.

I wrote the second book in about a week, The *Ecstasy You Want Heaven But Won't Give Up Hell*! I knew after I did that this was what I wanted to do more of. I felt it was the right time and space.

I remember going on Craigslist to search for production gigs. I did a few productions as an extra in Georgia, but I wasn't trying to make a career of it. I wanted to be behind the camera and work more as a producer or writer than an on camera talent.

Can you believe I ended up landing a script from Craigslist from a well-known producer/director/writer? Getting that gig was at the right time. It encouraged me to stay in my field. After he got the script from me (that he still admits he never read, haha), he called me to help him produce a Gospel play with well-known singers at the Fox Theater!

I was thrilled. I jumped at the chance, and when the production was done, we worked on other projects, but the job I had was short-lived. There were fewer projects, and I needed to pursue something. I started a radio broadcast on an AM station in Georgia for about eight months.

I was venturing into bringing the show to tv at a local station. Every week, I had to create new content, find guests, and create promotional material. It was taxing, and I was so focused on production, content creation, and working freelance gigs that burnout was brewing.

When I got overwhelmed by working and not seeing the sales, I thought I would shrink back out of production and media. This industry can pull a lot of your time and energy. The big checks are what we all pay attention to, but the moments where we don't sleep, work from one gig to the next, and create for no pay are the things kept secret. Every day is not the best day, and some days, you can feel a constant pull with no clear direction forward.

I needed rest, so I went back to the brook and sat. I needed the rain to come. Perhaps I was doing what we all can do. See the rain coming and think I just need to run to it. I can see it, so it is close. Only as you chase after the sky, clouds move, and your feet falter long before catching up. I was drained and starting to get in my head again.

I started to think maybe I was wrong to choose production, writing, and media. I was good at working with my hands and talking to people. Maybe I needed to do more of that. So, I went into a field where I could make money and didn't have to use my brain. I know it sounds sad, but I went to hospitality. If you have a sweet spirit, care for people, and customer service skills, you can do well as a server.

Chapter 9

Scripture from Proverbs 6:6-8

Now, my last serving job was before Covid. I stopped serving in 2018 and only a few times in early 2019. As I waited tables, my joy was returning. I found love in the simple things. The mist I needed, I got it when people smiled. When children were so polite, or people complimented me, it brought me the confirmation I needed to know that I was special. I enjoyed seeing people happy with their families and helping them to have a good time by keeping their glasses full and the food coming!

Life was simple, and I didn't miss what I had left at all. I was running to find peace, and I found it. I was being renewed. I never went anywhere, so it would be a surprise, I guess if I found time to meet someone outside of the restaurant. We got along fine, although our ambitions and follow-through were different. He was a great server, kind, fun, and charismatic. Our boys have his charm and good looks. He was more than a pretty face, though. He has a heart to do well, although he can struggle with that same virtue often.

We got married and had our first son. I took time off when I reached my eighth month. Before I stopped working, I sat down frequently to allow my body time to catch up from all of my movement. Maybe it was the weight of the baby, but I'm not too sure. They thought he was going to be larger than he was, too.

At this job, moving around constantly, lifting trays, and doing things started to impact the progression of my delivery. I frequently was losing my breath and just didn't feel like myself. I prayed about if I should keep going or take my leave.

There was no pay when I was gone. I had no job because I wasn't working on the side. But I was good at saving. So, I had savings that I leaned on for the time when I didn't work. It was during this time my brook went dry. Not because I ran out of money but because I was brought back to the assignment.

I went off into the flowers, but the Father said, that's enough, Krystal. You good. You healthy. Time to get to work. During that time, between giving birth to my son and him growing, I determined to start my production and publishing business.

Rain that Waters New Life

I started editing books for people. I got my office in Georgia, renting from a mayor who had space available. The price was incredible, and it was just what I needed to get focused again.

It was up a steep set of stairs, so my body got the workout for sure! The noise was gone, the sun was out, and I saw what the rain was watering. I started getting clients, and I had enough business not to need the restaurant job anymore. I tried to work a day a week, but I didn't do that for long.

My mother stayed with me and helped with my son when I was at work. When I had my office, my son came with me each day eventually. My mom came to help support me in the office and I loved having them there.

It was nice to be close to all of my children. My daughters went to a school around the corner, B Tutored, with Mrs. Beverly and her sister. It was a great time. I kept this office for a year. Then, life began to shift again. As I was creating content of my own and helping others, I realized I didn't need the space anymore. Most of my work was online so shifting to connecting with people online just made sense.

I separated from this husband because we were having issues. He had some things he wanted and needed to do, and our age gap didn't help. He needed more time to mature in his career choices and romantic commitment to marriage.

I got a three-bedroom apartment, and you would have thought that two incomes would have helped me sustain it. Although he tried to move in with me and drain time, God had saturated my house. All the bills were paid, my children were good, and my mother didn't have any lack. I worked from home, and things were going well and upward.

At the tail end of 2019, I got my doctorate in philosophy with an emphasis in Theology and was ordained as a chaplain. After that, I was focused on doing more ministry–even more than before. I spent more time studying than working, it felt like. I had wonderful dreams. Some I have seen, others still to be seen. I had a light heart open to hearing from God.

Upon moving into this apartment, I also found out two months prior that we were pregnant again. This is my fourth child, second son, and I was back to being alone. I had no help from my second daughter's father, and my sons' dad needed me more financially than I could rely on him.

It was the infidelity that sent me packing fast in the other direction. It would have been different if it had been outside my house, but for it to be in my house was more than I could deal with. He and I have been struggling for the past year and a half with infidelity. So it was a punch to the gut, but it didn't bring a storm.

Some relationships seem to tear up your life

Rain that Waters New Life

when they end. Others work to be fertilizer for what the rain will use to grow something the Father has for you. It was hard to see him and my mother bicker back and forth. It was strange to see his actions of isolating family members who I believe had my best interest at heart.

I didn't agree with a lot of what he said and did, but I was faithful in respecting him even if he didn't do that for me. Not because he deserved it, it was just right. When we are doing what is right, we may not always feel that the sun is shining and confirming us. Sometimes, it is us humbling ourselves to allow the Father to get the honor.

This was that kind of thing. I knew it was ending, and I wasn't sure if it was permanent or temporary. There is plenty more of course, from both marriages, but what you do with your experiences is a point of greater reflection for me. I share the growth I have accomplished through splits and divorce, not to glorify these life cycles but to show if you are battling in your marriage or working to be respectful when you want to take over and control; God WINS!

I was wiser than my second husband. I had more experience with life than he did. Yet, I let him be the man he wanted to be. There are choices we make and those the Father prefers. The test we must go through and the lessons we must learn. I don't regret my past, although the outcomes can leave a stain of pain. But there is a Cleaner who can wash the stained garment and remove all the presence of pain and failure.

I believed in redemption, reconciliation, and moving forward. Rain can mean the promise of new life. I know that when things are slow, we can look for the back door. So I didn't want to exit too early. Things can happen, and life kept changing.

Although my personal life was in shambles, I refused to allow that to impact my spiritual and personal life. I knew that this was a distraction, that his coming and going was not to be my focus. I could love someone but keep my distance if the direction they are choosing is not in the will of God. It's okay not to know the answer, but where God stops, I would stop, too.

I was pregnant and had several months still to go. I worked from home on books and helping clients. Even as I reflect now, I am not sure of where the money came from. I don't recall working many jobs. I don't have a chain of books that came out.

What did help me substantially during this time was that I was in a car accident where someone hit me and totaled my vehicle. That payment was issued, and that was how I lived for several months. The payment wasn't that large either, but how simple I lived, it took care of us for almost the year.

When I get my taxes back, I don't spend any of that money. I save it because I know the year can be filled with surprises. I use my taxes to supplement my income, so if I have a drought, provision is there. During this year, I had no worries or stress. I never chased money or got thirsty for clients, even when I could use the money.

I trusted God no matter what it looked like, and He always gave me what I needed. At times, I had tens of thousands and others a thousand. My faith in Him didn't scale because of the numbers I saw. I knew that He was my source and would provide all my needs.

My health with my second son was fine overall, but I developed a Bartholin cyst that steadily enlarged. It started off as no big deal, and I could function just fine. As the days and weeks went by, I started to feel more pain when I did anything. I wasn't a complainer, and I felt it would go down on its own. So I endured.

How often do we have a small problem that we ignore because the pain is bearable, that we don't address it? I didn't address this cyst for I don't know how long, and the cyst grew to the size of an avocado! It was so large I could not walk. I tried home therapies, and one day, I refused to complain, so I remember singing gospel music lying on the floor.

I heard my mom say, "Krys, you alright?" In tears, I responded, "No…" She asked what was wrong, and I didn't want to alarm her. I was ashamed to show her even though she was my mother. Funny,

I know, but it was the reason I held out this long. But when she saw it, I saw her eyes and knew it was bad.

She said, "Naw, baby, you need to go to the hospital." I didn't want to. I didn't know what was going to happen. I had faith to believe I could be healed, too. So I wasn't sure what the right thing to do was. How many of you know God can use doctors to heal? They can play a role in His miracles.

I had a dream about a week ago. In the dream, I was 32 weeks pregnant, and I was in the hospital. The doctor was in a panic, and I was on a stretcher, I guess. Everything was moving quickly, but I saw myself pushed through double doors and heard, "This baby is coming now!" I woke up scared.

I rebuked the dream because I wasn't sure of its purpose. Days after that, I was lying on the floor singing praises as I didn't know what else to do. I tried hot presses and everything. Nothing worked.

The ambulance came, and they had to pick me up because I couldn't get up. They sat me down in the seat and pushed me out of the house. My children were so concerned, and I hated to alarm them all. They were so sweet and asked, "Mommy, are you okay?" "Is everything going to be alright?" Through my pain, I tried not to cry, and I said, "Yes, Mommy is fine." But they knew I wasn't fine at the moment.

My mom said to them, "It's alright, tell Mommy bye for now. She will be back laughing!" They said bye and kissed me. Then, I had to be carried down a flight of stairs because the cyst was what I was sitting on, and it was huge.

The bumps would have sent me in even more pain, and I was grateful for their willingness and strength to carry me. Do you need someone to carry you through your troubles? I felt like the man on the mat being brought to Yashua (Jesus) in the Bible by his friends (Mark 2:3-11).

Anyhow, I was transported to the hospital, and there the doctor was pretty quick to see me. She came into the room and asked how things were I told her "not good." She asked my pain level, and I said an 8. Although this thing was terrible, I knew there were other things that felt worse. Yes, I was in tears, but if I had to go longer, I could have, but I didn't want to.

She asked if it was okay for her to look and I said, "Please." She looked, and her eyes went so large, and she said, "Wow, I have never seen one this big, ever. How are you able to walk?"

"I stopped being able to today."

"How long has it been like this?"

"Maybe a few weeks. It was small, and then it just started getting bigger lately."

"For you, don't you ever wait to get this looked at. The pain you are in could have had you abort your baby."

There it was! The dream I had was a warning about going to the hospital to get this addressed, and if not, it would have been to bring my son into the world premature. I was beyond thankful. Six weeks later, at 38 weeks, I gave birth to my second son, Nathan.

This was during Covid, so there were restrictions on how many people could be in the hospital. My husband and I at the time were trying to figure things out. I remember when my water broke for the first time ever. He was such a simple birth; all my other pregnancies, the doctors had to break it for me.

When I saw that he would come, I knew I had a few hours, if not longer, before any action would happen. I went to the grocery store and made sure my children had what they needed. I played a little bit with my son. My sister watched them for me when I went to the hospital.

I got into the car and drove myself to the hospital. My mom had already moved to Indianapolis, so she wasn't there. It was good also because I wanted to be fair and invite my mother-in-law to be there. She wasn't at the birth of Ayden, so I wanted her to be here for Nathan. So I parked across the street, took my ticket, and walked to the ER. "Hi, I am here to check into Labor and Delivery."

Rain that Waters New Life

"Do you need a wheelchair? Anybody come with you?"

"No, I can walk, thanks." I walked up to the floor, and they must have thought I was crazy because I was so calm. I didn't even know how far I was dilated when I arrived. I got geared up to have my fourth child, and they said, "You are five centimeters dilated. Looks like you will be having a baby!"

I was excited and ready to go. My mother-in-law came in time, but unfortunately, because of the rules with Covid, I didn't want to take a Covid test and stick anything down my nose to scrap my throat–it was all scary to me, she couldn't enter the room where I had my c-section. I could have had him vaginally, but I didn't want to wait. Two, my tubes were getting tied, and I wanted it all done at once.

I think it is odd you have a c-section wide awake. I heard Nathan and knew he was fine. It was a relief and a joy to hear his voice. He came out light just like my other children. Over the next few days, as his color kicked in, I got scared when I saw him have what looked like blue lips. I Googled it and was like no, can my baby not breathe!

My mom said, "I don't think it is that. He's just getting his color. Look at his ears. See how dark they are. His body is just catching up." Sure enough, about a few weeks later, he was chocolate all over.

Things with the husband didn't improve. I caught him at a hotel with a woman, and then he was staying out until the next day and all kinds of stuff. It was over, and it was time for me to take a break.

The baby was here, and my other children needed me. I knew I had to leave, so a month after my second son was born, I visited Indianapolis to see if I would move there or to Texas!

Scripture from Exodus 34:21-22

I moved from Georgia, my exodus, to Indy. Coming to Indy at first seemed foolish. I had a family but no job. I had an apartment I had to either cancel the lease or find a way out of. I needed to find a place to come here, and I didn't even have an interview set up! As I drove, there wasn't a cloud in the sky. That same breeze I felt when I went to Georgia from Florida, I felt on this road. I was praying and giving the Father glory as I drove the ten hours while my children slept.

When I first came for a week, I stayed with my Grandfather. He was kind to give us a room, and my mother allowed us to crash her space while I figured life out. When I first came, I spent the time praying and thinking a lot about what the Father wanted from me. I was close to my mom and family.

I was quiet during this time and didn't speak much online or be present anywhere. I knew decisions were up ahead, but I refused to have fear move me to make decisions. I had four children and a couple of thousands left from my settlement, which I got back in January of this same year. It is now September. My son was just over a month old, and I was nervous to leave him with anyone, not family.

When I came to visit someone I had not seen in years, since I was a child, I saw her again. My Auntie Wendy! She is naturally my cousin because she is the cousin of my mother. It seemed odd to call her by her name or even Cousin Wendy, so I asked to call her Auntie Wendy. She agreed, and we have been growing a relationship, with me being much older than before.

She and her son were a Godsend to my family. She said if I were to move here, she would be open to watching my children for me if I needed her to. She loved them all when she first met them. She put my heart at ease, and now my prayers could widen from where to live to when to move!

I loved that my family was here and I could have support here. I considered moving to Texas because I thought opportunities might be plentiful there, too. Only there was a big storm that took out their power one year that put those planes on ice. Plus, I wasn't interested in driving another ten hours from where I arrived. It would be Indianapolis that I would make a second home.

No Clouds in the Sky

I started looking for a job because I knew I needed that to get approved for housing. The only issue to truly move was that I needed housing and a job. My grandfather's place was too small, and to stay a week was about all they could do with my children and me. I am sure they would have given me more time, but I never want to wear out a welcome by good people! Even from family members.

When I made up my mind to move, I was still on the fence when I was driving home. There was still much to be sorted out. I needed a way out of my lease because if I broke the lease, that would gobble up several thousands of dollars in the process. I wanted to leave with all that I had.

So I prayed about that, too. I needed a miracle, on a miracle, followed by a miracle. When I got home, it was dark. I didn't kick my husband out, but we slept in different rooms. I slept on the couch and gave him the bedroom since months prior. I didn't want to sleep in there and hadn't for some time.

Coming home and finding women's underwear didn't bother me at all. I wasn't surprised, but I was sure convinced that moving was best. He wasn't helping with the boys, and I needed support to keep things from falling apart. I needed someone who could share the load with me of watching the children, but he wasn't able or willing to do that. So, moving again, was pushed in my face.

I told him I was moving and that as soon as

I could leave, I was going. He was understanding, and we talked about plans for what to do moving forward. We agreed filing for divorce was the best thing. I filled out all the documents, and he and I signed at the courthouse the same we got married (it was in a different county). We both understood the marriage was over, and he had moved on, so I should do the same.

The marriage took time to finalize. I also waited a year to see if things could get turned around before I pursued the divorce wholeheartedly. So, getting to Indianapolis, I moved into a weekly hotel. We stayed at the hotel for two weeks because staying longer would be costly. I knew that meant I had fourteen days to get a place and move our things out.

We had a double-bed hotel room that housed me, my four children, and my dog Joi. Joi was the sweetest dog to us, not good with strangers, but loving nonetheless. It was light staying in this hotel on my heart.

My children were happy, and I was at peace. I was applying for jobs when I was in Georgia. I didn't get any interviews confirmed while I was there. But a miracle happened!

I would walk the complex with my dog Joi, and as I walked, I would pray. I love walking amongst the trees because my apartment complex was beautifully decorated. So, walking the sidewalks was fun, therapy, and alone time for me and God.

No Clouds in the Sky

I prayed on this day like before, but something felt different. Have you ever felt rain and there wasn't a cloud in the sky? It wasn't a despised rain but a welcomed refresher.

Something I noticed when I got home was that the floor was wet near the AC unit. I thought for a second that the water from the fish tank might have overflowed when I was gone. I checked all around it but didn't see that as the reason for the moisture. I took photos of the water and I spotted it! A mushroom was growing from my carpet!

I immediately told management and said I could no longer live in the apartment and would be leaving immediately. They said I could move, but they were still requiring me to pay the buyout clause. I asked for management and sent an email with photos to verify the incident.

Maintenance came and confirmed the issue. All the while, they are fighting me about leaving, I am packing. I packed a three-bedroom two bath house in less than 72 hours. I didn't sleep for two days to get everything done!

I not only packed the house in boxes, I also had to rent the U-haul, breastfeed my son, feed my children, and throw the trash away. I had to put my furniture on Craigslist that I wasn't taken. I sold my couch, bed, children's beds, dining set, and anything else that couldn't fit between my van and a trailer I hitched to my van. My van didn't have a hitch when

I bought it, so I had that installed.

I never drove a hitch before. It was a quick learning curve on how to swing this trailer to land in the right place. I felt like I was going to cry many times, but the clock was clicking. My family was busy; my children helped as much as they could, but they had to sleep. I was on prayer, and strength was given from on high because I shouldn't have been able to pull it off.

I got everything in the van, emptied the trash, and was able to carpet-clean the house before turning in the keys by 6pm EST. The senior manager told me that if I could be out by 6pm, then she would waive the fees, and if not, I would have to pay for another month. As soon as I dropped off the keys, I headed out of the complex and drove straight to Indianapolis! As I started to drive, I looked at my phone and saw an email. The email asked if I could do an interview the next morning at 9am.

Can you imagine? I was on my way into town and would get there only an hour before I had to get dressed and head to an interview! I drove the trip with no stops, but only to fill up and take anyone to the bathroom. For the most part, they were asleep the entire trip. I got to the hotel, checked them in, and had to head off to this interview.

I was so fresh to Indy that I couldn't take the hitch off before the interview. I took up two spaces to park straight because I learned that backing

No Clouds in the Sky

up wasn't as easy as it sounded. The interview was quick, and I thought it went well. I left there and left the results in God's hand. I went to the hotel and slept three hours before I got a call from my mom.

"Hey, Krys. How's it going?"

"It's going. We are here. I am so tired."

"I have a favor to ask."

My mom's brother's dad had died a few days before I moved to Indianapolis. He was the stepdad my mom loved growing up. Grandpa Jimmie, she would call him. I met him once when we came to Chicago when we were children. He was kind and gave us dollars. He was a smart businessman, who always kept money, and took care of my mom when she was young.

She asked if I would drive her three hours away to the funeral. I wanted so badly to say "no" so I could sleep, but I packed my children back into the van that still had our stuff in it and headed to my grandfather's house. I asked, "Granddaddy, do you know how to get this hitch off? I cannot keep driving this thing around." He laughed and agreed to take it off for me.

Seeing that thing removed was like taking weave out of your head, light. It makes you recognize how much you love your hair, even if it is short when you remove it. It was nice to have someone awake to help me drive this time. My mom doesn't drive on highways, so I drove there and back, but she talked and kept me up. We didn't spend the night, so it was a whole day on the go.

As we enjoyed the memorial, it was nice to get a surprise call while we were at the reception. I answered, and it was the company that I had interviewed with earlier. They told me they wanted to offer me the manager position and asked how soon I could start. I said, "Monday!"

It was a wonderful celebration to enter the weekend knowing I had a job. It was a good thing because my tire went flat and I had to get a spare tire the next day. I squared all of my children away with my aunt, and I was ready to start. The job was to work with an online school that targeted nurse students.

I worked in this position, and I saw some flaws in their practices early on. I wasn't certain how many issues there were because I was new. Within 30 days, I was running the department almost single-handedly. Most of the staff was under-performing, getting sick with Covid, or taking other positions. Sales reps were lying to customers and expecting us to cover their mistakes.

On top of that, this company hated giving refunds or canceling contracts. I thought it wasn't good business to mislead people and then saddlebag them with a debt. For them to buy a program they could not use, especially for new students, seemed unfair. I tried to help everyone. The school wasn't trash, of course, but it could have had some improvement. I knew my time there was numbered because I wasn't confident in the product like when I started.

I stayed to help the people who I knew were interested in the service and those who were deserving of a refund. In 60 days, I was the department head and reported to the vice president, the owner's dad. The lady who hired me, I had her position. Only, there was nowhere else to go in the company I cared to go. Honestly, I didn't care to stay in the position.

The staff I helped to hire accused me of not listening to them. Although my style of communication is listening in silence, and then I repeat what you say, then I comment. They then said, "Yes, I communicate well, but I don't listen to them." They were all employed for less than 30 days and were bringing their ideas from other companies. They didn't want to learn the position. They just saw a vacancy as manager and thought to be the department head, perhaps.

I wasn't mad. I knew my days were numbered a month ago. Funny, when you pray about things, and the Father tells you a date, and you hear it, it can take you aback a bit. The date I heard in my head that was clear as day was my last payday. It was a wonderful occasion because it proved I could hear Yah, and I knew He was close to me.

I had someone tell me not to look them in their eyes because they felt I could see into their soul. Another who said I was insensitive because I asked them if they were okay when they were sitting at their desk crying loudly. She said I made her feel as if I was making fun of her. Yet I never mentioned her problem, never asked to pray with her, but I prayed about her problem.

She talked more about her personal affairs in the office than I thought was appropriate, but I didn't mention that. I was the new girl. Then, a coworker bought everyone flowers and left me out. I didn't care. I got my check, and that was enough for me as long as I could help people. My productivity spoke for me.

I got to be second in command in 60 days, so I was okay with being out of this company in 90 days. I remember the vice president told me, "Your kind was lucky to have a person like me." Unsure of how to respond but fully knowing the intent, I replied, "Thanks." I exited the office as quickly as I could.

He told me when he let me go that it wasn't my work ethic or productivity but that I was not a "mother hen." So you know I have to write a book on this subject. You know for me, a mother is not a person that prevents you from being responsible for your actions but the latter. I got more to say, again, *Mothering Spirit* has my thoughts rooted in biblical truth, of course.

No Clouds in the Sky

It wasn't all bad, of course; there were nice people, and I absolutely loved my manager and a woman I helped hire. We speak from time to time. When I left this job, I said to the Father, "Here I am. What are we doing next?"

You would have thought I would start looking for a job. I didn't. In fact, I haven't had a job since. I have been working for my dreams ever since. I wanted a fashion and cosmetic line, so I started it. I used lines of credit to get things going, and it was a bust, but I learned a lot!

I went back to writing and publishing. Here is where the flow came. I realized that being in alignment can shield you for even when things go off the railings. I had no job, started a business that failed, but none of my bills were late.

My husband came back for a month but got caught up in much of the same thing. He left with a Dear John text, didn't say bye, but left at like 3am or a thief in the night. He said he was paying the rent that month, but I had it the whole time. I just didn't voice that I did to see what he would do. He ran and never looked back.

It was okay, though. The Father paid the rent and utilities, bought the food, and took care of it all! I am still living off the blessing, and the outpour is evident in my life!

The outpour, the overflow, is not limited to

what happens to me or for me. To me, the outpour is expecting the Lord to make all things work for my good! If you believe and Trust Him, He will not let you down!

Scripture from Matthew 13:30-39

Aren't you glad that the Father allows the wheat and the tares to grow together? For some of us, we were a tare sown amongst the wheat. We were displaced and not living up to what God wanted from us. We were doing our own thing, causing our own destruction. Some of us were planted in places we didn't belong. What if you are not part of the weeds, but you are the wheat planted in the wrong place?

What if people labeled you a weed because they didn't want you to impact others? Do you know the plants people call a weed, like the daisy, have health benefits? Mullet that grows from the ground can help with breathing problems, but many States spray it and kill it yearly. If only you knew the essence of your story and the importance of your life, maybe you wouldn't be so quick to want it cut down. You won't let others cut you down, but you would fight to be counted amongst the wheat, the Children of God.

If you feel down low and out of it, I am a witness. Yah, God Almighty can change it. He doesn't need you to have it all figured out. He already has a plan for your life. This plan was established before the foundation of the world. You are vital and important in ways that, if you give it a chance, you will see.

When I didn't have a family, I still believed in it. When I didn't have a job, I still thanked the Father for income. When my businesses were slow and when I lost money, I trusted God. When jobs came and went, I believed He was my source. When I had no one to turn to, when I saw things leave out of my possession, He gave it right back with increase!

Don't let the cares of this life rob you of your confidence and trust in God. He is bigger than cars, jobs, spouses, income, and what you stand to gain and lose. My soul has learned to be content in plenty and want; I am anxious for nothing. I don't see things as they can be worse. I see it as what all the Father can make great! I make room for miracles in my life so they come again and again.

The Father loves for us to lean and depend on Him. He is a loving Father here to direct our path and show us His mercy is new everyday. When I make mistakes, He shows me how He covers me. When I lose sight of what is important, He will sit me down and renew my strength.

If I get off track with praying, studying, or being mindful of Him, He knows how to silence the noise. As you make room for him to enter into the places you need Him most to change for your life, you will find Him. He is the Great I AM, which means anything you need, "I Am!"

May you continue your journey from here and be encouraged to start your business, write your book, pray for your family, believe he can overcome your mistakes, and redeem your time! Your life is not over! For many of us, it has only begun. Welcome to the outpour! Where everything you need, can imagine, and believe for will happen with you here or dead and gone. If you have money or not. Realizing He is your source gives you unlimited access because He is not outmatched by anything.

Lean into Him today for whatever you need, and see Him appear mighty in battle. I would love to see you in one of my books, which can help you take the next step in your journey. Here are a few I recommend based on your next step in your personal growth process. If you need services like personal coaching, new business services, publishing, or something else, I have a short list of resources to follow on the next page you can use. Again, wonderful job for completing this book. Bye-bye for now.

Spiritual Growth:
Bless the Works of My Hands 21-Day Devotional
Release Pain (40 Day Devotional)
The Embrace Your Crown Series (3 books!)
- Open 7 Gates to Find and Overcome Heartbreak
- Open 5 Gates to Overcome Unbelief
- Open 3 Gates to Sharpen Your Focus

Christian Fiction (Novels that Inspire)
Leaking
The Gray Space
The Monster
We Expect Drip, Not the Downpour
The Alone But Never Lonely Series

Children's Books
Put Your Helmet On
The Weight of the Elephant
Loves You
Samantha's Greatest Gift
The Lesson Series for Youth and Teens (10 books!)

Books for Him (Husbands/Sons)
The Biggest Mistake Can Cost You Everything
Rise and Fall of King Saul
The Ecstasy
Over the Fact

Starting a Business: Turn Key Solution: (Series)
- Go From Dreaming to Paid
- Nail Your Sales Goals: Books & Services

Writing & Publishing Your Book Easily! (Series)
- Write Anything Easily (Books & E-Books)
- Creating the Perfect Story (Novels, Scriptwriting, Audio books)

Shop Books from AuthorKLee.com

Shop all titles and get access to free bonus offers at AuthorKLee.com or use the QR.

Use Promo Code:

Drip

Redeem at: AuthorKlee.com

About the Author

"God blesses those who work for peace, for they will be called the children of God." Matthew 5:9

K. Lee is a strong believer in prayer and believes the Truth sets anyone free. She is grateful that the Almighty has come into her life and removed her from a path of self-destruction to one that keeps her heart, mind, and desire to help the masses. As a child, she wanted to be light-hearted and not wear her heart on her sleeves or not cry when she saw others cry. This, however, was not the way the Lord made her.

The Lord called Krystal to have a heart that cares for others, sympathizes with the afflicted, and seeks justice or help for the needy. K. Lee is passionate about projects that build up people, remove oppression and pain, and deliver hope. Her childhood ambitions were to express her thoughts and those of the silent in music, dance, theater, and especially in writing.

K. Lee has written over 30 books and has a goal to publish at least 50 or more! Her books are both fiction and non-fiction, spanning seven genres: adult, children, youth fiction, self-help, spiritual growth, novels, business, empowerment, etc., to help people in their most profound times of need.

She is also passionate about coaching programs and web courses she created for WAE (Write Anything Easily) Process, Embrace Your Crown, Turn Key Solution for Small and New Businesses, Transform Go Beyond Change (Personal Development, and The Lesson for Youth and Teenagers.

In addition to writing books, K. Lee is passionate about video and media production. She started writing music and then transitioned to screenplays and theater. K. Lee is a talented actress who prefers to be behind the scenes.

Dr. Lee is equally passionate about ministry as she is about commerce, entertainment, and writing. She enjoys teaching and speaking on subjects relative to her life experience and anointed ability. She believes God has a calling on her life to be a mouthpiece for Him; she is prepared to follow His voice and travel to where He sends her without the slightest hesitation.

K. Lee hates religion, spreading faith through fear, and believes in the value of men no matter the current condition. No one is beyond the healing hand of Yahweh if they want the help. Help can be offered but must always be accepted, which requires choice. Yahshua is her Lord and Savior, and she looks forward to His coming. The days we live in remind her that The Second Coming is growing near. She believes and is passion-

About the Author

ate about helping all who have an ear to hear the Good News!

If you would like to learn more about K. Lee (Dr. Lee) or order more of her published books, you can find her online using the information below.

FB, TW, IG Pages: @AuthorKLee
AuthorKLee.com
DrKrystalLee.com
Me@DrKrystalLee.com
me@AuthorKLee.com

AuthorKLee.com
Creator of
WAE Process

    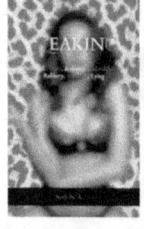 
   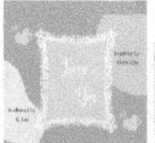  

SCAN ME

Call or Text:
770-240-0089 Press Extension 1
Web: KLEpub.com
Email Services@klepub.com

It's time to start and finish **YOUR Story**!

KLE Publishing specializes in helping people become authors. In as little as 15 to 90 days, we can help you develop your books and e-books and publish to 39,000 outlets! We also offer audiobook services.

Write, Edit, Format, Publish
We can help from
Start to Finish.

Explore and learn more about published authors affiliated with KLE.

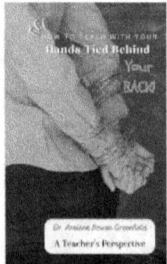

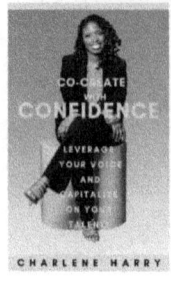

KLEPub.com

www.ingramcontent.com/pod-product-compliance
Lightning Source LLC
Chambersburg PA
CBHW070108080526
44586CB00013B/1235